Terri Susan Zurbrigg

X = What?

Terri Susan Zurbrigg

X = What?

Douglas Coupland, Generation X, and the Politics
of Postmodern Irony

VDM Verlag Dr. Müller

Imprint

Bibliographic information by the German National Library: The German National Library lists this publication at the German National Bibliography; detailed bibliographic information is available on the Internet at http://dnb.d-nb.de.

Any brand names and product names mentioned in this book are subject to trademark, brand or patent protection and are trademarks or registered trademarks of their respective holders. The use of brand names, product names, common names, trade names, product descriptions etc. even without a particular marking in this works is in no way to be construed to mean that such names may be regarded as unrestricted in respect of trademark and brand protection legislation and could thus be used by anyone.

Cover image: www.purestockx.com

Publisher:
VDM Verlag Dr. Müller Aktiengesellschaft & Co. KG, Dudweiler Landstr. 125 a, 66123 Saarbrücken, Germany,
Phone +49 681 9100-698, Fax +49 681 9100-988,
Email: info@vdm-verlag.de

Copyright © 2008 VDM Verlag Dr. Müller Aktiengesellschaft & Co. KG and licensors
All rights reserved. Saarbrücken 2008

Produced in USA and UK by:
Lightning Source Inc., La Vergne, Tennessee, USA
Lightning Source UK Ltd., Milton Keynes, UK
BookSurge LLC, 5341 Dorchester Road, Suite 16, North Charleston, SC 29418, USA

ISBN: 978-3-639-04593-2

1

Table of Contents

INTRODUCTION   **3**

The "Un"Enlightenment of Generation X   5

Jekyll and Hyde: Coupland's Competing Authorial Personalities   6

What is Generation X?   7

Filling in the Blanks: Coupland and "Blank Fiction"   9

Four Novels, Four Different Versions of Generation X   11

CHAPTER 1 – IRONY ON THE SIDE: THE PARADOX OF *GENERATION X*   **17**

Silent Sunrise: The Affective Challenge of *Generation X*   18

Waking Up from the American Dream: *Generation X* and Grand Narratives   22

Learning to Speak Again: Narrative Therapy and Recovery   27

Keeping Up with the Joneses the *Generation X* Way   29

Generation X Is Watching: Spectatorship and the Commodification of History   32

"We Gotta Get Outta This Place": Deserting the Desert   33

CHAPTER 2 – GET A HAIRCUT, AND GET A REAL JOB: *SHAMPOO PLANET* AND THE EXPANSION OF GENERATION X   **36**

"Yuppie Wannabes": Expanding Generation X   36

I Shop Therefore I Am: Consumerism as Defense Mechanism   37

Digging for History: Ironically Rethinking the Vietnam War Memorial   41

Keep the Platitudes Coming: Telethons as Ironic Signifier   43

Say It With Flowers: The Struggle for Sincerity in *Shampoo Planet*   45

Hollywood Squares, or, The Evolution of Success in *Shampoo Planet*   46

"Life at the Top": Tyler's Emotional, and Professional, Progress   47

CHAPTER 3 – GENERATION X AT WORK: *MICROSERFS* AND THE IMPORTANCE OF BEING 1.0   **50**

Bottomed-Out Boomers: Inverting the Demographics of Generation X   51

There Is a God, Bill Gates Be Thy Name: Microsoft as Pseudo-Religion   53

Machines with Paycheques, or, Life as a Microserf   55

Microserfs as Coupland's Critique of Corporate Culture   57

What Does it Matter? : Irony as Detachment   59

The Symbolism of Software: The Importance of Being 1.0   62

"Brought to You By": The Function of Commodification in *Microserfs*   64

An Ending Without Irony   66

CHAPTER 4 – IT'S THE END OF THE (POSTMODERN) WORLD AS WE KNOW IT:
GIRLFRIEND IN A COMA **68**

Comas: Medical Condition or Postmodern Pathology? 71

While You Were Sleeping: The Problematization of Progress 73

The End of the World Isn't Funny: When Irony Becomes Idiomatic 75

Narrative Channel-Surfing: Television and the Grand Narrative 76

Time for Plan B: Life After Irony 78

Are the Critics Jaded Too? 81

CONCLUSION: X = WHAT? **83**

BIBLIOGRAPHY **84**

Primary Sources 84

Secondary Sources 84

Works Consulted 86

Introduction

On June 9th, 2005, I went to the Canadian Centre for Architecture in Montréal, Quebec where Douglas Coupland was scheduled to give a talk to celebrate the opening of his "Super City" art exhibit. As I was not on the museum's exclusive list of invitees for the event, I arrived over two hours early in order to secure a place in line should a space should open up. While Douglas Coupland is a very well-recognized Canadian writer and artist, this sort of queuing is normally reserved for rock stars and other such celebrities. Nevertheless, such preparation was well rewarded: within 20 minutes of my arrival, the line behind me contained over 100 people, all clamouring to get a glimpse of Coupland. As not a single invitee failed to show up, we were all ushered into an ad hoc overflow room where we were able to watch a live video feed of his talk, the next best thing to being in the same room.

After, as I patiently waited for the book signing to begin, my thoughts wandered to Coupland's novels, not an uncommon direction for them to take considering I had spent most of my time since April writing a Master's thesis on *Generation X* (1991), *Shampoo Planet* (1992), *Microserfs* (1995), and *Girlfriend in a Coma* (1998), his first four works of literature aside from a collection of short stories entitled *Life After God* (1994). I was mulling over the research I had done for this project when it hit me: one would think that a figure who garners this much attention would have vast amounts of critical material written about him. However, this is not the case. As I had discovered over the preceding months, there was surprisingly little criticism that directly addressed Coupland's novels.

There are five books that circuitously address his writing, either devoting a chapter to one of his novels, or, due to the immense success of his debut novel, *Generation X*, by discussing him as the guru of this often misunderstood demographic born between 1965 and 80 (Martin 1). There is, however, not a single academic book devoted entirely to the work of Douglas Coupland. [1] After scouring journals and databases, I was able to find only six articles that directly addressed his novels, and four that did so indirectly, like the books, by referring to his work in a discussion about Generation X. Overall, criticism on Coupland focuses disproportionately on *Generation X*, his breakthrough debut, and *Girlfriend in a Coma*, his earnest, and controversial,

---

[1] At the time I submitted my Master's thesis in August, 2005, this statement was indeed true. However, the first book-length study of Douglas Coupland is scheduled to be released in 2008: see Andrew Tate, *Douglas Coupland* (Manchester: University of Manchester Press: 2008).

dismissal of postmodern irony. Consequently, my main objective in this book is to fill this void by providing the first comparative study that offers a detailed examination of Coupland's first four novels.

Ever since my first encounter with Coupland's work, he is a writer who has puzzled me: critics heralded him as a novelist "celebrated for his postmodern cynicism" yet, whenever I read one of his novels, its sentimentality reduced me to tears.[2] How could the novels of an author lauded for his sarcasm simultaneously be literary tear-jerkers? Determined to solve this conundrum, I set out to frame this problem in a more academic fashion, as I could hardly submit a grant proposal entitled "Why Douglas Coupland Makes Me Cry." Throughout the course of my research, I realized that the tension underlying Coupland's work, and the crux of my response to it, had to do with his complicated engagement with, and ultimate renunciation of, postmodern irony.

Before I explain this approach in more detail, I want to emphasize that this book is not about postmodernism, at least not directly. At first glance, it appears as though Coupland's writing, which addresses fragmentation, alienation, commodification, media domination – all the major "ions" of postmodernism – naturally invites a discussion about postmodernism. And to a certain extent, it does. For example, Frederic Jameson's theories about late capitalism, Jean-François Lyotard's ideas about the dismantlement of grand narratives, and Jean Baudrillard's work on simulacra, are all postmodern concepts that can be fruitfully applied to Coupland's novels.

However, merely arguing that certain aspects of Coupland's work in turn engage certain aspects of these scholars' theories does both parties a disservice. First, there is already an abundance of provoking and thoughtful commentary that examines Jameson, Lyotard, and Baudrillard in much more detail, and much more effectively than I am able to within the confines of this project. Moreover, an extended effort to grapple with the influential and complicated ideas of these theorists would overshadow my main objective, which is to provide a comprehensive overview of Coupland's novels, on which there is *not* an abundance of critical material.

---

[2] Tate, Anthony. " 'Now – here is my secret': Ritual and Epiphany in Douglas Coupland's Fiction." *Literature and Theology* 16.3 (2002): 326-38 at 326.

Mark Forshaw makes a very important distinction between being a postmodern novelist, and being a writer who engages with ideas associated with postmodernism. He accurately places Coupland in the latter category, arguing that he is "a novelist who writes *about* postmodernity."[3] He goes on to state that Coupland's treatment of postmodernism is one of "distaste for both its cultural and its economic manifestations."[4] Although the application of certain postmodern theories illuminates Coupland's work, a close reading of his novels unambiguously reveals that he is a writer who challenges this discourse more than he channels it.

The concept that underpins this thesis is irony rather than postmodernism. However, the two ideas are interrelated because the way in which Coupland's irony functions can only be properly understood in light of the cultural developments associated with postmodernism. While nearly every review that discusses Coupland's novels refers to his use of irony, few delve any deeper into this issue in terms of the overall significance of irony to his work. Coupland's relationship to irony is a fraught one indeed, and it is one that I spend the bulk of this book addressing. As Forshaw states, "what Coupland deplores, with growing conviction throughout his work to date, is a debilitating irony and cynicism" that seem to be the inevitable result of postmodernity.[5] Consequently, the ideas of Lyotard, Baudrillard, and Jameson are alluded to throughout this book because they shed light upon the elements of postmodernism that contribute to Coupland's antagonistic relationship to irony.

The "Un"Enlightenment of Generation X

One of the most common issues with which Coupland grapples in his novels is the idea of grand narratives: paradigms imbued with immense ideological power that "structure the discourses of modern religion, politics and philosophy."[6] An example of one such narrative is Jürgen Habermas's "Enlightenment Project," which involves the "intellectual quest to unlock the secrets of the universe in order to master nature for human benefit and create a better world."[7] This mission has sought to "improve human existence through technology."[8] Whereas the Enlightenment outlook is an optimistic one that assumes that "progress is inevitable,"

---

[3] Forshaw, Mark, "Douglas Coupland: In and Out of Ironic Hell." *Critical Survey* 12.3 (2000): 39-58, at 53.
[4] *Ibid.*
[5] *Ibid.*, at 55.
[6] Nicol, Bran, ed. *Postmodernism and the Contemporary Novel: A Reader.* Edinburgh: Edinburgh UP, 2002 at 16.
[7] Grenz, Stanley J. *A Primer on Postmodernism.* Michigan: W.B. Eerdmans, 1996 at 6.
[8] *Ibid.*

Coupland's novels undermine this teleology by pessimistically depicting a world that, despite the progress implicit in profound technological advancement, has nevertheless regressed into ironic alienation.[9] Writing novels that undermine the veracity of the Enlightenment grand narrative is an act that putatively aligns Coupland with postmodernism, a discourse that also eschews "the Enlightenment myth of inevitable progress" and "replaces the optimism of the last century with a gnawing pessimism."[10] However, Coupland's depiction of the erosion of grand narratives does not automatically ally him with Lyotard, who argues that the idea of postmodernism is inextricably linked with the dismantlement of grand narrative such as these.[11] Although *Generation X*, *Microserfs*, and *Girlfriend in a Coma* are novels that call into question grand narratives, they also explicitly depict the difficulties associated with such narrative disinheritance, such as severe alienation and a sense of purposelessness. G.P. Lainsbury evinces that the ironic shield adopted by members of Generation X is, at least in part, caused by the lack of narrative framework governing their existence: "[they] mask their sense of betrayal and hopelessness with cynicism. Everything is a joke when the master narratives of European history no longer serve to legitimate the way things are."[12]

Jekyll and Hyde: Coupland's Competing Authorial Personalities

Ryan Moore argues that a byproduct of the "predominance of ironic distance" so rampant in contemporary society is a sense of "desperation, a longing for depth and meaning," a rather sentimental yearning in a world characterized by its cynicism.[13] Coupland's work oscillates between these seemingly antithetical polarities, a juxtaposition that confounds many of his critics. Jay McInerney characterizes these competing tendencies as Coupland's "dual authorial personalities."[14] It is necessary for Coupland to adopt this "narrative split-personality," because it is a strategy that enables him to portray the elements of postmodernity he finds most

---

[9] *Ibid.* at 4.
[10] *Ibid.* at 7.
[11] Lyotard, Jean François. *The Postmodern Condition: A Report on Knowledge.* Trans. Geoff Bennington and Brian Massumi. 1979. Minneapolis: U of Minnesota P, 1984 at 28.
[12] Lainsbury, G.P. "*Generation X* and the End of History." *Essays on Canadian Writing* 58 (1996): 229-40 at 239.
[13] Moore, Ryan. "And Tomorrow Is Just Another Crazy Scam': Postmodernity, Youth and the Downward Mobility of the Middle Class." *Generations of Youth: Youth Cultures and History in Twentieth Century America.* Eds. Joe Austin, and Michael Nevia Willard. New York: U of New York P, 1998. 335-36.
[14] McInerney, Jay. "Geek Love." *The New York Times.* 11 Jun. 1995: 1-3. *Lexus-Nexus.* InfoTrac. MacLennan Library, McGill University, Montreal, QC.. 01 Nov. 2004, at 1.

problematic.[15] The transition from irony to earnestness reflects Coupland's overall mission to repudiate postmodern irony, a trajectory he gradually follows in his first four novels. Coupland's Jekyll and Hyde act underscores the paradox of his writing because he is a novelist whose work exemplifies tenets of postmodernism while at same time staging "a direct attack upon some key postmodern truisms."[16]

What is Generation X?

Sociologically speaking, the term Generation X refers to the demographic born between 1965 and 1980 that due to its inauspicious position as the successors of the dominant Baby Boom generation is at an economic disadvantage.[17] In the 1990s, however, Generation X emerged as a concept with a panoply of meanings. As Douglas Rushkoff, author of *The GenX Reader* claims, "Generation X means a lot of things to a lot of people. We are a culture, a demographic, an outlook, a style, an economy, a scene, a political ideology, an aesthetic, an age, a decade, and a literature."[18] Appropriately, the letter signifying this generation is the same letter used in algebraic equations to indicate the unknown, the unclear, what remains to be answered.

Douglas Coupland is the author most commonly associated with Generation X due to the title and subject matter of his debut novel, *Generation X: Tales for an Accelerated Culture*, published in 1991. In that same year, Generation X emerged rather suddenly as a media phenomenon. As Oake observes, "prior to 1991, no one in the U.S. mainstream media talked about Generation X . . . and then, almost overnight, Generation X became one of the most talked about subjects in the U.S. media."[19] Also released in 1991 was Nirvana's breakthrough album *Nevermind*, and Richard Linklater's cult status film *Slacker*, respectively characterized by Rushkoff as the album and the film that best captured Generation X.[20]

While he is often credited with having coined the term Generation X, the label had been in circulation prior to Coupland's debut novel. According to John M. Ulrich, the term Generation X was first employed in the early 1950s in a book written by Robert Capa which sought to

---

[15] *Ibid.*

[16] Forshaw, *supra* note 3 at 40.

[17] Martin, Catherine E. et al. "Perspectives on Generation X." *Popular Culture Review* 8.2 (1997): 109-19 at 109.

[18] Rushkoff, Douglas. *The GenX Reader*. New York: Ballantine, 1994 at 3.

[19] Oakes, Jonathon I. "*Reality Bites* and Generation X as Spectator." *The Velvet Light Trap* 53 (2004): 83-97 at 83.

[20] Rushkoff, *supra* note 18 at 3-5.

document the ways in which those in their twenties coped with the traumas of World War II.[21] Accordingly, the connotations of Capa's project suggest that the term Generation X has always signified a "group of young people, seemingly without identity, who face an uncertain, ill-defined (and perhaps hostile) future."[22] In 1964, Charles Hamblett and Jane Deverson wrote a book entitled *Generation X*, which provided a sociological study of British youth subcultures. Consequently, since the 1960s, the term "has continued to be closely associated with subcultural negationist practices and their often conflicted relationship to mainstream consumer culture."[23] Outside of the academic realm, prior to the release of Coupland's novel, people also may have known Generation X as the name a mid-1970's punk band in which Billy Idol played before launching his solo career.[24]

Paul Fussell's conceptualization of Generation X in his 1983 book *Class: A Guide Through the American Status System*, hints at some of the most prevalent themes explored in Coupland's novel. Fussell claims that "X people constitute something like a classless class. They occupy the one social place in the U.S.A. where the ethic of buying and selling is not all-powerful."[25] Notably, Coupland has cited Fussell's book as a source of inspiration for *Generation X*, particularly, the book's last chapter, "The X Way Out."[26]

While statisticians suggest that the members of Generation X inherited a world robbed of much of its promise and opportunity because of the demographic disadvantage that results from being the generation immediately following the baby boom, Coupland's work demonstrates that, additionally, they inherited a world fraught with the problems of postmodernity, as they were the first generation born and raised under the dominant influence of this discourse. While the media often characterizes Generation X as a demographic rife with detached and indifferent "slackers," Coupland's novels pose an explicit challenge to such a narrow and pejorative characterization by depicting characters who rail against rather than passively accept the potentially alienating irony that, for Coupland, characterizes postmodern society. While they are subjected to this cynicism, they refuse to be subjects of it.

---

[21] Ulrich, John M. and Andrea L. Harris, eds. *Gen-X-Egesis: Essays on Alternative Youth (Sub)Culture*. Madison: U of Wisconsin P, 2003 at 3.
[22] *Ibid.*
[23] *Ibid.*
[24] *Ibid.* at 10.
[25] Fussell, Paul. *Class*. New York: Ballantine, 1983 at 222.
[26] Rushkoff, *supra* note 18 at 16.

The concept of postmodernism adopted throughout this thesis is one closely connected with what Frederic Jameson calls "the cultural logic of late capitalism," a term he borrows from the scholarship of Ernest Mandel.[27] Jameson argues that the third and most recent stage of capitalism which coincides with and characterizes postmodernism, features "a prodigious expansion of capital into hitherto uncommodified areas," and this development is accompanied by "the rise of the media and the advertising industry."[28] For Jameson, postmodernism extends well beyond the realm of aesthetics, operating as "a cultural dominant" whose omnipresence is inescapable.[29] The psychological implications that arise from such a pervasive form of capitalism are alienation and emotional detachment, which Jameson refers to as "the waning of affect."[30]

Filling in the Blanks: Coupland and "Blank Fiction"

Building on Jameson's scholarship, Martin Annsley associates Coupland with a group of writers whose work he labels "blank fiction" because of its tendency to depict "the dynamics of contemporary capitalism."[31] According to Annsley, one of the most prevalent characteristics of blank fiction is its proclivity to "speak in the commodified language of its own period."[32] That is, the characters created by these writers demonstrate how the predominance of television, advertising, and other aspects of popular culture have resulted in a late capitalist vocabulary, one whose idiom is necessarily ironic and whose lexicon is commercialized. Rushkoff characterizes this co-opted language as an expected, though nevertheless pernicious, byproduct of commercial culture: "Like any youngsters, we learned the language we were taught when we were kids, it just happens that this is the language of advertising."[33] Coupland's *Generation X, Shampoo Planet, Microserfs,* and *Girlfriend in a Coma* support this assertion in that they feature characters who appear to be deprived of a language not tainted or previously co-opted by advertising. It is difficult to speak without a smirk, or without wincing, when nearly everything uttered sounds like a slogan, or seems to be borrowed from a sitcom or a film. This is why Umberto Eco characterizes communication in the postmodern realm as speaking "in an age of lost innocence":

---

[27] Jameson, Frederic. *Postmodernism or, the Cultural Logic of Late Capitalism.* Durham: Duke UP, 1991 at 13.
[28] *Ibid.* at 37.
[29] *Ibid.* at 22.
[30] *Ibid.* at 26.
[31] Annesley, *Blank Fictions.* London: Pluto, 1998 at 7.
[32] *Ibid.*
[33] Rushkoff, *supra* note 18 at 5.

the sheer impossibility of saying something genuine means that all utterances are couched in irony.[34] The cynicism inextricably linked to postmodern irony thus becomes reflexive.

The role of television has changed profoundly in the postmodern era. While in 1961 Allan Ginsberg composed his long poem "Television was a Baby Crawling Toward That Deathchamber," a mere 20 years later, members of Generation X would chant "I Want My MTV."[35] Coupland's characters, who "were born into an age where mass media reaches into every aspect of life, have never really known reality unframed by mass media and are consequently unable to avoid relating everyday 'real' experience to everyday fictional experience, especially that which has been screened."[36] The pervasiveness of television in this regard has had an indelible impact on language and its capacity for sincere, untainted expression. As Lawrence R. Samuel maintains, "television advertising quickly emerged as a new vocabulary all Americans could share."[37] Each chapter in this book discusses the role of television in the commodification of language and the way in which Generation X's "physical and linguistic space has been colonized by the discourses of mass media" poses an immense challenge to the ability of its members to communicate effectively.[38] The realization that language has been co-opted by advertising is one that undoubtedly fuels the irony that permeates the worldview of this generation.

While Annsley's ideas regarding the commodification of language in late capitalism provide a deeper understanding of Coupland's novels, his ideas about Generation X merit further consideration in terms of their relationship to Coupland's work. That he associates Generation X with the "nihilistic worldview" which characterizes most blank fiction demonstrates how Generation X has been discursively constructed as an apathetic generation rather than an active one.[39] Coupland's fiction flouts this stereotype. *Generation X, Shampoo Planet, Microserfs,* and *Girlfriend in a Coma* are all works that depict characters who, demographically, are members of Generation X. However, Coupland goes against the grain by portraying these characters as

[34] Eco, Umberto. "Postmodernism, Irony, the Enjoyable." 1985. *Postmodernism and the Contemporary Novel: A Reader.* Nicol, Bran, ed. Edinburgh: Edinburgh UP, 2002. 110-13 at 111.
[35] Mills, Katie. "'Await Lightning': How Generation X Remaps the Road Story" in Ulrich, John. M. and Andrea L. Harris, eds. *GenXegesis: Essays on Alternative Youth (Sub)Culture.* Wisconsin: U of Wisconsin P, 2003. 221-49 at 226.
[36] Nicol, *supra* note 6 at 4.
[37] Samuel, Lawrence R. *Brought To You By: Postwar Television Advertising and The American Dream.* Austin: U of Texas P, 2001 at ix.
[38] Nicol, *supra* note 6 at 5.
[39] Annsley, *supra* note 31 at 3.

individuals who try to overcome the apathy and ironic detachment that is such an integral part of the society in which they were raised. Slackers and nihilists do not behave in such an oppositional manner. His characters' attempts to transcend postmodern irony also contradict Annsley's declaration that blank fiction is "uncommitted," serving mainly as an exemplification of the postmodern condition.[40] While Coupland's writing does provide an overview of late capitalism's pernicious influence on contemporary society, the explicit desire to repudiate postmodern irony that permeates his fiction suggests that perhaps his inclusion in Annsley's list of blank fiction writers is somewhat misguided.

Four Novels, Four Different Versions of Generation X

Generation X represents Coupland's first step towards a repudiation of postmodern irony. The novel itself tells the story of Andy, Dag, and Claire; three twenty-somethings who undergo what Daniel Grassian calls "a postmodern, existential crisis in which they realize their essential meaninglessness or emptiness."[41] As the generation that succeeded the Baby Boomers, the members of Generation X found themselves at an enormous professional and economic disadvantage as the domination of the job market by the Baby Boomers left them with limited, and often undesirable, employment prospects.[42] Such stunted opportunities make it difficult for this generation to believe in the narrative power associated with the American Dream grand narrative, a storyline that promises to reward diligence and hard work with material success. Such promises have not come to fruition for Andy, Dag, and Claire. The alienation "brought on by the failure of consumer society to provide them with a stable or fulfilling identity," ultimately causes them to seek refuge in the California desert.[43] This retreat, which I refer to as "desert detox," affords them the introspection that their thwarted participation in the proverbial rat race does not. Faced with the ensuing alienation of a disingenuous grand narrative, Andy, Dag, and Claire adopt a policy of "bedtime stories."[44] This routine enables them to develop a narrative that more adequately accounts for their experience, while at the same time, provides them with a safe space in which they can shed their wry armour and express themselves by sharing their emotions and their fears, an exercise in sincerity of which the late capitalist realm has deprived them.

---

[40] *Ibid.* at 4-6.
[41] Grassian, Daniel. *Hybrid Fictions.* New York: McFarland, 2003 at 86.
[42] Lainsbury, *supra* note 12 at 234.
[43] *Supra* note 41 at 86.
[44] Douglas Coupland. *Generation X.* New York: St. Martin's, 1991 at 11.

Irony plays a paradoxical role in *Generation X*: while it is the destructive force from which the protagonists seek refuge, its inescapability is something that Coupland addresses vis-à-vis the side-bar definitions that appear throughout the novel. Ostensibly, these sarcastic sound bytes shed light upon the lifestyle and habits of Generation X. What they actually do, however, is incorporate into the novel the glib irony its protagonists attempt to evade. Using D.C. Mueke's theory of "double irony," chapter 1 discusses at length the ways in which Andy, Claire, and Dag's mission is undermined by the presence of these definitions.

Generation X serves as an important starting point in Coupland's novelistic trajectory because it establishes two elements central to an effective understanding of his work. First, it illustrates his desire to transcend postmodern irony, a cultural condition his characters frame as an illness from which they need to recover. Although the presence of the ironic side-bar definitions undermines their journey somewhat, the final pages of the novel, which describe Andy's experience of a transcendent, emotional moment, are devoid of these definitions, thereby suggesting that *Generation X* represents Coupland's first, albeit tentative, steps towards a repudiation of postmodern irony. Second, true to its title, *Generation X* addresses the issues often associated with this demographic: limited job prospects, financial difficulties, and the alienation that results in being the first generation to come of age in a late capitalist realm. As the later chapters of this book reveal, as far as Coupland is concerned, Generation X is more of a concept than a demographic, and it is a concept he revisits and revises at length, turning many media stereotypes on their head in the process.

If *Generation X* is a novel that establishes the intense need, however doomed, to flee from postmodern irony and the late capitalist realm that contributes to it, then *Shampoo Planet*, discussed in chapter 2, establishes just how pernicious, and pervasive, this irony is by depicting it at length. The protagonist of *Shampoo Planet* is Tyler Johnson, an ambitious, convivial twenty year-old who, despite his demographic status as a member of Generation X, remains determined to land a high-flying job at a corporation. Tyler epitomizes a teenager raised in a commercial society as he is convinced that success can be purchased if only he buys the right hair products, clothes, and accessories. Shopping is how he quells his anxiety not only about his limited potential for advancement as a member of Generation X, but also about his diminished capacity for emotional involvement. Tyler's tendency to imitate a talk show host whenever he has something serious to discuss exemplifies both Jameson's notion of waning of affect and Eco's theories about how communication in the postmodern era is necessarily steeped in irony because discourse has been preemptively commodified by advertising and other forms of media. Ultimately, *Shampoo Planet* provides an overview of the "intensively commercialized culture that has been identified as one of the defining features of late capitalism" that the characters *Generation X*, *Microserfs*, and *Girlfriend in a Coma* strive to resist.[45]

The way in which *Shampoo Planet* ironically revisits many of the more earnest moments of *Generation X* further demonstrates how it is a novel that exemplifies postmodern irony more than it problematizes it. For example, whereas Andy is disconcerted about how history has become commercialized and, consequently robbed of its authenticity, Tyler embraces this trend by suggesting that history should be considered a "theme park" people pay to visit. Although the characters in *Shampoo Planet* tend to embrace the very elements of contemporary culture reviled by the protagonists of *Generation X*, Tyler nevertheless undergoes a transformation similar to that of Andy, Dag, and Claire, albeit on a more subtle plane. He still defies his demographic position by landing a job at Bechtol Corporation, but the final pages of the novel show him steadfastly struggling to abandon the ironic layer in which his conversations were previously couched in favour of a more genuine register. *Shampoo Planet* thus provides an important reconsideration of the characteristics of Generation X established in the first chapter. While issues such as "boomer envy" still loom large, chapter 2 demonstrates how Coupland's second novel provides a more nuanced portrayal of this generation by creating a character who is not disenchanted with commercial culture, but, for the better part of the novel, embraces it, as well as the American Dream grand narrative that it sells.

Continuing his constant rethinking of the Generation X paradigm, *Microserfs*, Coupland's third novel and the focus of chapter 3, offers an even further departure from the characteristics frequently associated with this demographic. *Microserfs* tells the story of seven friends who gradually come to the realization that their menial, albeit lucrative, jobs at Microsoft are turning them into human versions of the computers they work with. After an epiphanic discussion that leaves them convinced that their toilsome positions are causing them tremendous psychic and physical damage, they quit and move to Silicon Valley in order to work for *Oop!*, a start-up software company founded by a fellow Microserf. *Oop!* is a company whose product and philosophy are diametrically opposed to that of Microsoft. While Microsoft primarily makes

---

[45] Annsley, *supra* note 31 at 126.

software that helps people be more productive in an office, *Oop!* makes software that encourages the creativity associated with leisure rather than the productivity associated with the workplace.

The deification of Bill Gates featured in this novel signifies how in a late capitalist realm, technology and corporations provide institutional surrogates for religious devotion in a secular society devoid of such narrative frameworks. The type of irony addressed in this novel stems mainly from the complete alienation the Microserfs feel while working at Microsoft. In a pivotal scene in the novel, the protagonists try to destroy their "Ship It" awards, which they receive to celebrate their productivity. So detached are they from their work, and so miserable does it make them, that the very item that signifies their success at work becomes a lightning rod for the ironic detachment that makes their (lack of) personal lives so unpalatable.

While the Microserfs' paycheques and material successes potentially undermine their status as GenXers, their attempt to find a salve for the ironic alienation they feel, combined with their awareness of and concern about the trappings of a commercial society, arguably re-establish them as such, thereby reaffirming that for Coupland, members of Generation X are not defined by their jobs, but by their desire to transcend postmodern irony. *Microserfs* represents a step forward in Coupland's quest to repudiate irony because unlike *Generation X*, where the protagonists' desire to eschew irony is problematized, the attempts of the Microserfs find an environment unscathed by this ironic alienation is a clear success. Such a development implies that the pervasiveness of irony is somewhat weakened.

Girlfriend in a Coma, addressed in chapter 4, is Coupland's most controversial novel to date. In it, he abandons what Tate refers to his "slacker realism" and moves into the realm of metaphysics.[46] While critics such as Philip Marchand consider *Girlfriend in a Coma* to be a rather abrupt paradigm shift for an author who once provided the snide, sarcastic voice behind the glossary that appears in the margins *Generation X*,[47] I argue that *Girlfriend in a Coma* represents the culmination of Coupland's novelistic trajectory rather than a digression from it. Although his adoption of a pseudo-biblical framework and his positioning of postmodern irony as a problem so severe only an apocalypse can destroy it seems like a dramatic departure from his three earlier novels, as the final chapter of this book demonstrates, *Girlfriend in a Coma*

---

[46] *Supra* note 2 at 325.
[47] Marchand, Philip. "Humbleness of the Heart." *Toronto Star* 21 Mar. 1998: M15.

contains many similar themes and offers the same renunciation of irony as Coupland's earlier novels, it just does so in more explicit and extreme terms.

Karen's character functions as a cipher through which Coupland communicates his anxieties about the postmodern world. After being in a coma for from 1979 until 1996, she miraculously awakens after seventeen years and she when she does, she provides a rather damning commentary about how the world has changed during her prolonged absence. While she is asleep, Karen's friends live through these changes, and the ironic jadedness they develop as a consequence renders them impervious to the cultural shifts Karen perceives immediately. Although Karen's awakening from the coma seems like an unlikely event, what follows is even more shocking: the world ends with a catastrophic flood that strongly resembles the Noah's Ark parable of the Bible. Before this cataclysmic event, the world's entire population, save for Karen and her friends, falls into a symbolic coma that signifies late capitalist alienation and detachment. The behaviour of Coupland's characters in the aftermath of this postmodern apocalypse demonstrates why Coupland felt such an event was necessary in the first place. Rather than ruminate upon the significance of their role as survivors, or contemplate why the world ended in the first place, they revert to the commercial comforts of watching movies and fantasizing about celebrities. This affectively challenged behaviour which speaks to the contemporary dependency on popular culture continues until Jared, the ghost of their friend who died of leukemia as a teenager, reappears in the guise of an archangel who informs them of their chosen status as those who will carry out "Plan B," an undertaking that seeks to rid the postmodern world of its dependence on irony. Suddenly, the characters' lives have meaning and purpose because instead of remaining apathetic and disengaged, they are charged with the duty of questioning the world, and consequently becoming actively involved in it rather than alienated from it. In *Girlfriend in a Coma*, Coupland puts an end to the postmodern irony that plagues the characters of his earlier novels, irony that they attempt to transcend to varying degrees of success.

Each chapter in this book provides a discursive space in which I explore how the members of Generation X, as Coupland portrays them, cope with the implications of eroded grand narratives, the struggles associated with building new ones, and the anxieties of identity involved with late capitalist subjectivity in which irony is the most prevalent, but also the most problematic, idiom. That he positions Generation X as a demographic that resists, rather than reverts to, this cynicism explicitly challenges the widely held notion that "Gen Xers incorporate irony into all situations, conversations, and lifestyles."[48] As the novels considered in this book demonstrate, the opposite is true.

---

[48] Moore, *supra* note 13 at 255.

Chapter 1 – Irony on the Side: The Paradox of *Generation X*

My objective in this book is to trace Coupland's gradual espousal of sincerity and sentimentality in lieu of the wry alienation that plagues postmodern existence. This chapter demonstrates how *Generation X* represents the paradoxical beginning of this endeavour. At first glance, *Generation X* does not look like a novel. Rather, it resembles a guidebook in which the main text, in this case a story about three troubled twenty-somethings, is surrounded by a glossary of definitions, slogans, and sometimes cartoons. Such formal aberrations are not surprising given that *Generation X* was initially conceptualized as "a nonfiction handbook of Gen X behaviours and attitudes."[49] In this regard, these side-bar definitions featured throughout the novel ostensibly shed light upon cultural phenomena unique to the Generation X experience. I argue however that their role is much more complex, and crucial, than merely providing the reader with additional information on this often misunderstood demographic. While this interspersed glossary often ironically illuminates the events of the novel, it also undermines the protagonists' attempt to provide a steadfast critique of the trappings of commercial culture. Andy, Claire, and Dag's desire to replace their ironically detached worldview with a less contaminated outlook is challenged by the presence of these wry, reductive definitions which commodify their experience by packaging it in a commercialized, reader-friendly format. How can a quest be unique and subversive if it is accompanied by advertising slogans?

G.P. Lainsbury's assertion that "irony is the dominant mode" of *Generation X* is indicative of the critical assessment of the novel overall.[50] Although critics are quick to affix such a label to this work, none has explained exactly how irony operates in this novel, or for that matter, in Coupland's work more generally. When characterizing *Generation X* as an ironic work, many critics cite the terminology that appears in the margins as evidence.[51] While sardonic in tone, these definitions do not in and of themselves render *Generation X* an ironic novel. Rather, it is the way in which they operate alongside the text, and how they function within the novel's overall structure, that makes them so. Despite the fact that the central narrative posits irony as a force harmful enough to require the characters to move to the desert in an attempt to escape its pernicious influence, there remains a palpable irony that permeates the pages of

---

[49] *Supra* note 12 at 232.
[50] *Ibid.* at 237.
[51] Forshaw, *supra* note 3 at 50.

Generation X. What then, is its source? The answer to this question lies not only in the content of the definitions, but also in their significant positioning alongside the text.

D.C. Mueke's theory of "Double Irony" provides an appropriate lens through which to interpret how irony functions in *Generation X*. He states that "ironies of this kind . . . take the form of paradoxes, dilemmas, or what we call 'impossible situations' . . . the ironist or the ironical observer himself feels the paradox or dilemma as a real one".[52] In this case, the inescapability of the commodity culture is the "impossible situation" Coupland addresses. One reason why Coupland decides to deploy irony in this way is perhaps because he himself is all too aware of the ironic futility of his protagonists' objective: is it really possible to successfully repudiate consumer society? Echoing Adorno and Jameson's theories about the inescapable ubiquity of "the culture industry," Ulrich claims that in cases where "no 'authentic' individual identity can be expressed, because it is always already mediated through commodities, self-conscious irony emerges."[53] Consequently, the structural irony Coupland employs in *Generation X* is a manifestation of such self-conscious irony: while the novel speaks to the oppressiveness of irony and depicts characters who try to reduce its pernicious omnipresence, he is, on one level, aware of the naivety that underscores their putatively alternative lifestyle.

It is no accident that much of the ironic humour found in *Generation X* is located along the margins, at a safe distance from the narrative, because that is exactly the realm to which Coupland and his characters want to relegate irony: outside their immediate discourse. As Martin Annsley observes, "in response to what they regard as the alienating materialism of the modern world," Andy, Claire, and Dag "try to withdraw from it and find a space untouched by its seemingly degraded influence."[54] While the story that unfolds in *Generation X* is one that depicts their attempts to elude such irony, the presence of the novel's marginalia, and its reductive, sarcastic nature, undermines their intentions by presenting their experience as another set of ideas that can be consumed, labeled, and commodified.

Silent Sunrise: The Affective Challenge of *Generation X*

The scene early in the novel in which the three protagonists watch the sun rise is one of the most poignant in *Generation X* because it introduces the problematic relationship between

---

[52] Muecke, D.C. *The Compass of Irony*. London: Methuen, 1969 at 25.
[53] *Supra* note 21 at 20.
[54] *Supra* note 31 at 118.

irony and sentimentality, an issue Coupland grapples with in all his novels. When confronted with the beauty of the sun as it "rises over the lavender mountain of Joshua," rather than comment upon it, the characters sit there in silence, "a bit too cool for [their] own good," paralyzed by their cynicism, uncertain of how to appropriately acknowledge the gorgeous natural event.[55]

There are several theoretical explanations for their behavior, including those provided by Coupland's ironic marginalia. One viable explanation for their stunted sentimentality is Jameson's idea of the "waning of affect," a detached emotional state that, in his view, is central to postmodernism.[56] He claims that the fragmented subjectivity associated with postmodernism results in "a liberation from every other feeling" as well.[57] He qualifies this fatalistic statement somewhat by stating that people are not "utterly devoid of feeling," in today's society, but that their ability to develop and express their emotions is challenged due to the "impersonal" nature of the contemporary realm.[58] He argues that such alienation is furthered by a "reified media speech" that compromises the capacity of language to be sincere.[59] The ultimate result of these psychological byproducts of late capitalism is the predominance of "a 'seen it all' cynicism."[60] The resulting tendency to "do, say, and feel nothing" is exemplified by the protagonists' silence when watching the sunrise.[61] They yearn to say something about this momentous event, but find themselves unable to do so as they have just recently departed from a realm in which the sincerity of language and the genuineness of emotions has been all but "exhausted."[62]

Coupland provides a more tongue-in-cheek explanation of his characters' behaviour vis-à-vis the term "*DERISION PREEMTPION*," which is defined as "*a life-style tactic; the refusal to go out on any sort of emotional limb so as to avoid mockery from peers.*"[63] In an attempt to avoid being mocked for saying something that would inevitably sound fatuous due to the co-opted and commodified condition of language, Andy, Claire, and Dag sullenly appreciate the beauty of the sunrise in silence. While this "lifestyle tactic" is one his characters strive to leave

---

[55] *Generation X, supra* note 44 at 7.
[56] *Supra* note 27 at 26.
[57] *Ibid.*
[58] *Ibid.* at 27.
[59] *Ibid.*
[60] Moore, *supra* note 13 at 253.
[61] *Ibid.* at 254.
[62] *Ibid.*
[63] *Supra* note 44 at 150.

behind, in order to do so, they have to minimize their reliance upon a concept closely linked to derision preemption, that of "**KNEE-JERK IRONY**: *The tendency to make flippant ironic comments as a reflexive matter of course in everyday conversation.*"[64] He adds that "*avoiding knee-jerk irony is the main goal of Derision Preemption.*"[65] This definition further accounts for their silence because it establishes how, should they dare to speak, not only do they run the risk of sounding insincere, but they also risk mockery.

While on one level the sunrise scene demonstrates the extent to which Andy, Claire, and Dag have internalized a late capitalist viewpoint, it is also of pivotal importance because it establishes their desire to transcend this affective paralysis. The protagonists of *Generation X* are not happy or complacent sufferers of this emotional disorder. As Claire states, the "carapace of coolness" that envelops them must be broken because it is simply "not healthy to live life as a succession of isolated little cool moments."[66] The use of the word "carapace" is telling because it refers to a shell, or a protective covering, thus suggesting that irony is a type of shield or defense mechanism.

Andy, Claire, and Dag adopt two methods in order to escape from this irony. The first is geographical, and the second narratological, and both are encapsulated by Andy's statement that "this is why the three of us left our lives behind us and came to the desert – to tell stories and to make our own lives worthwhile tales in the process."[67] Their move to the Californian desert signifies their physical removal from the confines of commercial culture. As Annsely states, "the desert provides a seemingly uncontaminated environment, a place where economic imperatives have no influence, a space in which a kind of unalienated knowledge can be developed."[68] Andrew Tate further underscores the discursive implications associated with the protagonists' decision to take refuge in the desert by framing their journey as a recreation of "the oldest European-American sacred story: the journey west by a group hoping to find sanctuary and sanctity or a new Canaan that might accommodate a persecuted people."[69] Just as "separatists and Puritans abandoned the corruption of England to find a new land, one without the taint of

---

[64] *Ibid.*
[65] *Ibid.*
[66] *Ibid.* at 8.
[67] *Ibid.*
[68] *Supra* note 31 at 199.
[69] *Supra* note 2 at 330.

history," Andy, Claire and Dag move to the desert to eek out an existence free from the oppressive of irony and the commodified culture of late capitalism.[70]

According to Ulrich, the desert is an optimal place for the protagonists to seek refuge because it "functions as a metaphoric X . . . as a blank space within which the main characters will now attempt to inscribe a coherent narrative of their lives, a new identity."[71] Such an observation also heightens the resonance of the novel's title as *Generation X,* in this light, could refer to their demographic situation as well as their geographic location. The arid climate of the desert is symbolic indeed because for Andy and his friends it signifies a place where irony has dried up, where capitalism and consumerism do not flow freely, and the only thing germinating is the stories they tell about their lives.

Andy explains how their decision to "live small lives on the periphery" where there is "a great deal in which [they] choose not to participate" was motivated, in part, by the frustration of unfulfilling jobs: "Our systems had stopped working, jammed from the odor of copy machines, White-Out, the smell of bond paper and the endless stress of pointless jobs done grudgingly to little applause."[72] As Oakes contends, such an oppressive environment "provides the necessary point from which the *Generation X* characters yearn for something else – a place where the sarcasm, irony, cynicism and apathy of contemporary consumer society may disappear and return to them their 'lost purity.'"[73] Fortunately, Andy claims that since their decision to move to the desert, "things are much, *much* better."[74]

By comparing the protagonists' need to tell their stories to like-minded friends to Alcoholics Anonymous, Andy frames their decision to repudiate consumer culture in terms that imply they are giving up a of toxic drug or lifestyle, and that recovering from such a dependency necessitates a support group:

> Thus inspired by the meetings of the Alcoholics Anonymous organization,
> I instigated a policy of storytelling in my own life, a policy of 'bedtime
> stories,' which Dag, Claire and I share among ourselves. It's simple: we
> come up with stories and we tell them to each other. The only rule is that
> we're not allowed to interrupt, just like in AA, and at the end we're not

---

[70] *Ibid.*
[71] *Supra* note 21 at 14.
[72] *Supra* note 44 at 11.
[73] *Supra* note 19 at 96.
[74] *Supra* note 44 at 11.

allowed to criticize. This noncritical atmosphere works for us because the three of us are so tight about revealing our emotions. A clause like this was the only way we could feel secure with each other.[75]

His invocation of AA is doubly resonant. While in aligning his group with AA, Andy is suggesting that they suffer from a detrimental addiction, as Tate points out, AA is also a "group that continues to revere the significance and sanctity of narrative."[76] Because the protagonists of this novel feel narratively unmoored, it follows that they would embrace a discourse that privileges stories.

When viewed in the context of this explanation, their decision to move to the desert is analogous to the decision to check into a detoxification centre, one that prescribes narrative therapy as a pivotal aspect of recovery. This treatment requires them to tell stories, ostensibly about random people, but really about their own lives, as a way to imbue their existence with meaning, to situate them within an applicable and relevant narrative framework that has been denied them. As Claire frankly states, "Either our lives become stories, or there is just no way to get through them."[77] While perhaps not as broad in scope as a grand narrative, these micro-narratives serve a similarly important purpose: rendering their seemingly fragmented lives meaningful and whole. For Andy, Dag and Claire, the purpose of this "therapeutic, oral story-telling regime" is that it satisfies the "need for their existence to be legitimated by reference to a narrative that would make sense of it."[78] Because they are unable to see themselves in the American Dream grand narrative, it is not surprising that many of their tales "concern alienated individuals" who, like them, are unsure of how their lives are supposed to unfold in the absence of a narrative framework.[79]

Waking Up from the American Dream: *Generation X* and Grand Narratives

Douglas Rushkoff bluntly describes the unfortunate demographic quandary in which the members of Generation X find themselves as follows:

---

[75] *Ibid.* at 14.
[76] *Supra* note 2 at 329.
[77] *Supra* note 44 at 8.
[78] *Supra* note 12 at 235.
[79] *Ibid.*

> GenXers live in a world we feel is geared to people ten to thirty years
> older than ourselves. We watched as baby boomers went to college, got
> great jobs, crashed the economy, and left nothing but . . . low-wage,
> menial employment, or 'temping' – for their vastly overqualified little
> brothers and sisters.[80]

Such angst corresponds with the term "**_BOOMER ENVY_**," one of the many Generation X concepts Coupland defines in the margin of the novel: "_Envy of the material wealth and long-range material security accrued by older members of the baby boom generation by virtue of fortunate births._"[81] Critics such as Lainsbury affirm that the slim pickings left for Generation X is a function of demographics: "it is by now a truism among economists that young North Americans can no longer count on surpassing their parents' standard of living, that, in fact, they would be lucky just to equal it."[82]

Coupland's characters are no strangers to this particular breed of animosity. Early in the novel, Andy describes how his friend Dag abandons him mid-conversation so he can "scrape a boulder across the front hood and windshield of a Cutlass Supreme."[83] It is hardly coincidental that Dag engages in this act of vandalism after completing yet another late shift at "Larry's Bar." As Andy elaborates, "The car was the color of butter and bore a bumper sticker saying, 'WE'RE SPENDING OUR CHILDREN'S INHERITANCE,' a message that I supposed irked Dag, who was bored and cranky after eight hours of working his McJob."[84] Appropriately, on the right-hand margin of this page, the definition that accompanies this term appears: "**_McJOB:_** _A low-pay, low-prestige, low-dignity, no-future job in the service sector._"[85] Ultimately, McJobs, as Rushkoff exclaims, are all that remains on the economic landscape for Generation X as the Baby Boomers occupy the vast majority of desirable employment positions. Consequently, Dag is so provoked by this seemingly innocuous bumper sticker because from his perspective, the gentleman driving the car is not only depriving his own children of their inheritance, but he is also crassly flaunting the wealth of which he and his ilk have robbed Dag and his generation. If

---

[80] _Supra_ note 18 at 5.
[81] _Supra_ note 44 at 21.
[82] _Supra_ note 12 at 234.
[83] _Supra_ note 44 at 5.
[84] _Ibid._
[85] _Ibid._

any children are in need of inheritance, it is likely this fellow's. Dag declares that at times he wants to "throttle the [boomers] for blithely handing over the world to us like so much skid-marked underwear."[86] While perhaps not the most eloquent description of what Dag feels is his lot in life, such a simile aptly captures the resentment many members of Generation X harbour towards their parents, and about the "crappy" circumstances in which they find themselves trapped.

Dag's act of vandalism is, according to Andy, "merely one incident in a long strand of such events."[87] However, there is a method to Dag's madness: "He seems to confine himself exclusively to vehicles bearing bumper stickers he finds repugnant" such as "ASK ME ABOUT MY GRANDCHILDREN."[88] Dag's loathing of this particular bumper sticker reflects a different, more filial aspect of "Boomer Envy." Whereas the first referred to inheritance, hence smugly drawing attention to the wealth that Dag, as a member Generation X, may never acquire, the second bumper sticker boasts about family, an institution which, as a result of his limited prospects, may also prove elusive. Most likely, those in a position to advertise their progeny on bumper stickers have also attained a level of middle-class comfort that enables them to support such a family. This privilege may not be available to Generation Xers who, faced with bleak job prospects, find themselves in a state of arrested professional development. In a glossary appended to the novel, Coupland provides US Census Bureau statistics that reinforce the notion that it is in fact much less feasible for members of Generation X to get married and have families than it was for the baby boomers: between 1960 and 1987 the number of married people in the 30-34 age-group decreased by 20 percent, and while the percentage of income needed for down payment on a home increased by ten percent, the number of people in the same age-group decreased by nine percent.[89] These statistics, and Dag's outburst, demonstrate that it is a lot less likely he or his cohort will ever apply similar decorations to their automobiles (should they ever be in a position to afford one in the first place).

"Boomer Envy," however, does not always manifest itself through violent behaviour. Andy observes a less vehement exhibition of this phenomenon when he observes how his friends smile as though they have "been good-naturedly fleeced, but fleeced nonetheless, in public on a

---

[86] *Ibid*. at 86.
[87] *Ibid*. at 115.
[88] *Ibid*.
[89] *Ibid*. at 182-183.

New York sidewalk by card sharks, and who are unable because of social convention to show their anger."[90] This characterization effectively describes the socio-economic position in which many members of Generation X find themselves as they are at a demographic disadvantage they can do little to combat. Accordingly, Coupland coins a term that sardonically describes one strategy used to cope with this adversity: "*LESSNESS: a philosophy whereby one reconciles oneself with diminishing expectations of material wealth.*"[91]

Providing another, less extreme example of "Boomer Envy," Andy describes how he must endure his parents' insensitivity towards his inauspicious situation. Though well-to-do baby boomers, they nevertheless pretend that their financial situation mirrors that of their disadvantaged offspring. When Andy tells his mother that he wishes she "would stop coupon clipping, pretending you're poor," she responds by telling him, "Indulge us, Pumpkin. We *enjoy* playing hovel."[92] For the baby boomers, being hard up is an amusing game, but such simulations of poverty are not an option, but rather a reality, for their children. Prior to this episode, Coupland introduces the concept of "*SQUIRMING,*" which he defines as *Discomfort inflicted young people by old people who see no irony in their gestures.*[93] The wry juxtaposition of this definition and Andy's mother's comments is what Mueke refers to as "simple irony," a type of irony that seeks to wryly expose incongruency.[94]

Labelling it "one of the most evocative phrases in [the American] lexicon," Cal Jillson defines the American Dream as the promise that "those willing to learn, work, save, persevere, and play by the rules would have a better chance to grow and prosper in America than virtually anywhere else on earth."[95] Inherent in the notion of the American Dream is a grand narrative: it is a success story of mythological proportions which ensures that those who work hard will be materially rewarded. But, such a guarantee cannot possibly endure when demographic and economic conditions undermine its validity. As a result, the "sustained downward mobility" endured by members of Generation X "represents a threat to what has served as a crucial narrative."[96]

---

[90] *Ibid.* at 7.
[91] *Ibid.* at 54.
[92] *Ibid.* at 137.
[93] *Ibid.* at 112.
[94] *Supra* note 52 at 54.
[95] Muecke, D.C. *The Compass of Irony.* London: Methuen, 1969 at ix.
[96] Moore, *supra* note 13 at 259.

J.F. Lyotard declares that the central characteristic of the postmodern era is that "the grand narrative has lost its credibility."[97] Although the protagonists of *Generation X* demonstrate the veracity of this assertion, they simultaneously lament it due to the alienation than ensues. Although many postmodern writers felt "liberated" after the demise of the grand narrative due to the "experimentation" such discursive freedom permits, Coupland's characters feel stranded because they "appreciate the restorative power of narrative which has been lost in disjointed postmodern culture."[98] What they mourn more than anything else is the lack of an *applicable* grand narrative, because despite its continuing influence, the protagonists' demographic position as members of *Generation X* calls into question the viability of the American Dream.

On the one hand, through its depiction of "Lessness" and "Boomer Envy," *Generation X* contributes a healthy dose of incredulity to the American Dream narrative, a discursive "dismantlement" Lyotard associates with postmodernism.[99] On the other hand, however, that they feel alienated by this loss of a narrative framework which lends meaning to their lives undermines Lyotard's claim that "the nostalgia for the grand narrative is gone."[100]

Before quitting his job, Dag was doing everything in accordance with the American Dream plot. However, he was thwarted, not rewarded for his efforts. Not surprisingly, emerging from Dag's first attempt to express himself during "bedtime story hour" is the verbal cathartic equivalent of his vandalistic proclivities discussed earlier.[101] He regales his friends with a story about how he told off his baby boomer boss before quitting:

> Do you really think we *enjoy* hearing about your brand new million-dollar home when we can barely afford to eat Kraft Dinner and we're pushing *thir*ty? A home you won in a genetic lottery, I might add, sheerly by dint of your having been born at the right time in history? You'd last about ten minutes if you were my age these days, Martin. And I have to endure pinheads like you rising above me for the rest of my life, always grabbing the best piece of cake and then putting a barbed-wire fence around the rest.[102]

---

[97] *Supra* note 11 at 37.
[98] Grassian, *supra* note 41 at 91.
[99] *Supra* note 11 at 38.
[100] *Ibid.*
[101] *Supra* note 44 at 14.
[102] *Ibid.* at 21.

Appropriately, the following definition appears in the margins at this point in the novel: **VEAL-FATTENING PEN**: *Small, cramped office workstations built of fabric-covered dissassembleable wall partitions and inhabited by junior staff members. Named after the small pre-slaughter cubicles used by the cattle industry.*"[103] This wryly amusing definition adds sarcastic comic relief to what is otherwise a startling realization about the ultimate improbability of the American Dream grand narrative for members of Generation X. Moreover, the undermining of the American Dream as grand narrative adds another layer of significance to the notion of "Boomer Envy," because not only do members of Generation X envy the preceding generation their economic security and professional satisfaction, but they also resent how the boomers inherited a grand narrative that made good on its promise. This generation, on the other hand, will have to write its own script.

Learning to Speak Again: Narrative Therapy and Recovery

Narrative serves a therapeutic function in *Generation X* because using stories as a means of framing their opinions and concerns enables the characters to communicate. Although Dag's narrative about how he told off his clueless boss and moved to the desert is angst-ridden, it is important to point out how, in accordance with the narrative healing involved with "desert detox," he also frames his story in more emotional, vulnerable terms: "I was convinced that all of the people I'd ever gone to school with were headed for great things in life and that I wasn't. They were having more fun; finding more meaning in life."[104] This confession is safe within the confines of the friends' bedtime story ritual because the irony that pervades and perverts many other aspects of their lives is not permitted here. So secure does Dag feel from the "carapace of cool" that he feels comfortable discussing a notion as romantic and clichéd as "finding meaning in life" without fear of derision.[105] Framing his anxiety in such terms speaks to the power of narrative and the role it plays in rendering our lives comprehensible. Coming of age in a postmodern world that Lyotard glibly declares is rid of grand narratives, Coupland's characters are charged with the daunting task of inscribing meaning in their lives without these discursive aids.

---

[103] *Ibid.*
[104] *Ibid.* at 29.
[105] *Ibid.* at 15.

28

Later in the novel, when Dag places a troubled phone call to Andy and is at first unable to articulate what is bothering him, Andy instructs him to "make a *story* out of it."[106] Once Dag follows this advice, he is able to discuss his anxieties frankly over the phone rather than internalizing them or donning a shield of ironic distance.[107] Reasserting the shared desire of the characters to escape the rampant consumerism they fear is contaminating contemporary society, Dag's concerns involve his perturbation about the dominance of "mall culture."[108] So pervasive is this trend that dwelling places are no longer merely a means of shelter, but they have also been transformed into individual boutiques in which people showcase the commercial wares they have hitherto acquired. As he tells Andy, while on his journey "Otis got to thinking: 'Hey! These aren't houses at all – these are *malls in disguise!*'"[109] "Otis," of course, is a pseudonym for Dag. Fearfully, he tells Andy that like many shopping malls, these houses are located "about three feet from the highway," and take on the similar the shape of "blockish" brick buildings that are indistinguishable from one another.[110] Although he still needs the protection of an assumed name, his newfound ability to express his concerns in a genuine fashion rather than couch them in sarcasm and irony signals a significant development.

Andy's first bedtime story introduces a theme that is prevalent in all four novels discussed in this book: the distorted importance and resonance placed on consumer and popular culture. Whereas Dag leaves his job because he can no longer fathom working in a "veal-fattening pen," Andy abandons his previous form of employment due to his abhorrence of his boss's obsession with consumer culture. So wrapped up is this man in mass culture he considers a lewd photograph of Marilyn Monroe to be his "most valuable thing":

> he handed me a photo . . . of Marilyn Monroe getting into a Checker cab,
> lifting up her dress, no underwear, and smooching at the photographer . . .
> I was actually quite mortified that this photo. . . was his most valuable
> possession.[111]

---

[106] *Ibid.* at 69.
[107] *Ibid.*
[108] *Ibid.* at 71.
[109] *Ibid.*
[110] *Ibid.*
[111] *Ibid.* at 59.

29

The importance Andy's boss places upon this salacious photograph speaks to the disproportionate value placed upon celebrity. Astoundingly, the most important item in *his* life is a photograph of a woman he does not know personally, but rather one with whom he has become familiar by reading magazines or watching films. Such a distorted perspective is a prime example of Baudrillard's concept of the hyperreal, a realm wherein distinguishing between one's actual existence and the lives of celebrities and the characters they play becomes increasingly difficult.[112]

Andy makes even more progress than Dag in terms of sharing his emotions because while midway through the novel Dag still needs the safety net of a pseudonym, by the novel's conclusion Andy is "able to let his fictional guard down."[113] Upon beginning to relate a tale "about a young man," he stops and corrects himself: "oh get real, it's about me."[114]

Keeping Up with the Joneses the *Generation X* Way

A poolside discussion Andy and his friends engage in one afternoon exemplifies the veracity, and the implications, of Jameson's theories about "the prodigious expansion of capital into hitherto uncommodified areas."[115] In an attempt to promote an existence devoid of materialism and consumption, Elvissa, a friend of Claire's, asks everyone what "moment for you defines what it's like to be alive on this planet."[116] Before anyone answers, she adds an important qualifier to this question: "Fake yuppie experiences that you had to spend money on, like white water rafting and elephant rides in Thailand, don't count," thus exemplifying her disdain for the commodification of experience and memory that is a byproduct of late capitalism.[117] The consumerist realm from which these characters fled was one where so-called good memories could be acquired by spending money on an exorbitantly priced tropical vacation; where, rather than experience nature in a more authentic Emersonian fashion conducive to contemplation and self-analysis, one can experience artificial fulfillment with the help of a hired guide. It is precisely this type of paradigm that *Generation X* seeks to disavow. As Coupland's chapter titles

---

[112] Baudrillard, Jean. *Simulacra and Simulation*. Trans. Sheila Faria Glaser. Ann Arbor: U of Michigan, 1994 at 13.
[113] Grassian, *supra* note 41 at 92.
[114] *Generation X, supra* note 44 at 148.
[115] *Supra* note 27 at 37.
[116] *Supra* note 44 at 91.
[117] *Ibid.*

defiantly state, "Purchased Experiences Don't Count," because "Shopping is Not Creating."[118] It is intriguing that Elvissa equates experiences unsullied by consumerism with being alive, as such a statement implies that consumer culture, to her, represents a type of death. Similarly, to her friends, it represents an illness that requires desert detox.

Despite valiant efforts, relinquishing the detached irony that permeated their urban existence is an arduous process, and Dag's vitriolic reaction to Elvissa's spiritual retreat is one setback encountered over the course of their ambitious journey. Her departure for a more seemingly pristine environment hints at a discomfiting question that underpins *Generation X*: whether its protagonists are indeed the posers Coupland's side-bar definitions make them out to be. When Elvissa announces her decision to give up her already Spartan surroundings and go "one step further" by working as a gardener at a nunnery, Dag harshly mocks her.[119] In a display of knee-jerk irony, he snidely points out that her putatively pure destination publishes a "brochure," a type of advertising disguised as information, and sent her an "acceptance letter," thus implying the distinctiveness, or caché attached to her (perhaps purchased?) experience.[120] Dag's comments remind the reader of a definition Coupland provides a few pages earlier: ***CONSPICUOUS MINIMALISM***: *A life-style tactic [that involves] The nonownership of material goods flaunted as a token of moral and intellectual superiority.*[121] Dag's response to Elvissa's seemingly more aggressive pursuit of "conspicuous minimalism" recasts the protagonists' quest in a competitive and arguably condescending light. As Coupland's glossary points out, there is a fine line between "conspicuous minimalism" and "***CAFÉ MINIMALISM***: *To espouse a philosophy of minimalism without actually putting into practice any of its tenets.*"[122] Claire, offended by Dag's comments, accuses him of crossing this line:

> *You* should understand what it means to try and get rid of all the crap in
> your life. But Elvissa's gone one step further than you now . . . She's at
> the next level. You're hanging on still . . . to your car and your cigarettes
> and your long distance phone calls and the cocktails and the *attitude*. [123]

---

[118] *Ibid*. at 39, 87.
[119] *Ibid*. at 119-121.
[120] *Ibid*. at 120.
[121] *Ibid*. at 107.
[122] *Ibid*.
[123] *Ibid*. at 122.

The "*attitude*" to which she refers is the all-too-tenacious hold that the irony resulting from the belief that nothing is sacred or unsullied by commercialism still has on Dag, despite his attempts to overcome it. Ultimately, the implications surrounding this part of the novel echo the overall crisis, or "double irony," to reintroduce Mueke's term, that frames *Generation X*. Mark Forshaw further expounds upon this issue:

> a key problem in Coupland's first novel [is that] it takes the search for
> alternatives to American consumer culture seriously; [it is] a novel that
> invests the majority of its narrative sympathetically in the actions of
> characters who also take this search seriously. But, at the same time,
> *Generation X* is a novel that is conspicuously self-ironising, a text that . . .
> posits the sheer spatial *inescapability* of undermining irony.[124]

Regardless of whether their mission is doomed to fail, Andy, Claire, and Dag earnestly attempt to shed their ironic armour by continuing to take emotional risks even if they end up sounding sentimental or clichéd. Indeed, the ironic coating the margin definitions afford this novel is partially punctured by the touching, wholly sincere statements like the one Andy makes, notably, after the group's bedtime story hour:

> These creatures here in this room with me – these are the creatures I love
> and who love me. Together I feel like we are a strange and forbidden
> garden – I feel so happy I could die. If I could have it thus, I would like
> this moment to continue forever.[125]

Half of those statements could easily have been borrowed from cliché-ridden love songs or greeting cards. Yet despite the fact that those sentiments have been co-opted by Hallmark and the recording industry, these words capture his feelings and he expresses himself accordingly, without flinching. A latent question posed by the inherent irony associated with commodified language is whether it is better to risk expressing oneself in clichés or endure not being able to express oneself at all. Andy, Dag, and Claire indirectly answer that question by instituting a story ritual that encourages and enforces sincere communication. Indeed, cheesiness is explicitly sought after by Andy, who, like his friends, suffers from irony overload. He exemplifies this

---

[124] *Supra* note 3 at 43.
[125] *Supra* note 44 at 130.

yearning when he apostrophizes the absent Mr. Leonard, the photographer responsible for the taker the ancient (and inevitably cheesy) family portrait taken in his youth: "Oh, Mr. Leonard, how *did* we all end up so messy? We're looking hard for that *fromage* you were holding – we really are."[126]

Generation X Is Watching: Spectatorship and the Commodification of History

Understanding Generation X's relationship to history is crucial to understanding the commodified culture from which this generation longs to escape. Andy's trip to the Vietnam War Memorial poignantly addresses the implications of a generation whose relationship to history is heavily mediated by the visual media. As Andy's desire to visit the Memorial in the first place reflects, it is not only the lack of an applicable grand narrative he mourns, but also his compromised sense of history. As his younger brother Tyler says upon their arrival, "Andy, I don't *get* it. I mean, this is a cool enough place and all, but why should you be interested in Viet*nam*? It was over before you even reached puberty."[127] Andy's response is quite revealing:

> I'm hardly an expert on the subject, Tyler, but I *do* remember a bit of it. Faint stuff; black-and-white TV stuff . . . they were also the only times I'll ever get – genuine capital *H* history times, before *history* was turned into a press release, a marketing strategy, and a cynical campaign tool . . . I arrived to see a concert in history's arena just as the final set was finishing. But I saw enough, and today . . . I need a connection of a past of some importance, however wan the connection.[128]

Several critics have addressed the fraught relationship that Generation X has with history. Jonathan Oakes contends that it is one characterized by spectatorship rather than participation:

> being Gen X has something fundamentally to do with being a spectator in a way that being a baby boomer, for instance, does not . . . While boomers supposedly identify with the "actual historical event" signified by the image, Xers recall only the appropriation of this image by throwaway entertainment media. . . the implication seems to be that, for Generation X,

---

[126] *Ibid.* at 136.
[127] *Ibid.* at 151.
[128] *Ibid.*

the categories of "media" and "reality" have become fatally confused,
inverted, or perhaps dissolved altogether.[129]

Temporally, the end of the Vietnam war closely coincided with the emergence of
postmodernism's discursive dominance.[130] This coincidence in turn implies that the point at
which Andy perceives the "genuine" times of history ended is roughly the same time that history
began to be filtered through the mass media. One of the lasting significances of the Vietnam War
is that, as one of the first wars fought after the rise of television, it was also the first to receive
extensive media coverage.[131]

Lainsbury, borrowing from Marshal McLuhan's mantra "the medium is the message,"
argues that "[a]s children, members of Gen X might watch *The Brady Bunch* after school, and
then watch the fall of Saigon on the news with their parents over dinner. Each seemed equally
real or unreal, each had the same truth content."[132] Thus, because history is mediated through
television, its historical veracity and importance are difficult to discern as it is delivered in the
same format as commercials and sitcoms.

"We Gotta Get Outta This Place": Deserting the Desert

When Andy returns home from Christmas vacation, he discovers that Claire and Dag
have left for Mexico, with hopes of opening a hotel. It not surprising that a narrative depicting
their attempt to transcend irony ends with their departure from United States, the country which
Jameson argues played a pivotal role in implementing late capitalism.[133] Whether such a retreat is
a concession or a triumph remains ambiguous due to *Generation X*'s cryptic ending. En route to
join his friends in Mexico, Andy experiences an epiphany, the nature of which is closely
connected with Jameson's notion of the waning of affect. While he is driving, a large crowd of
people, among them a group of mentally handicapped teenagers, gather along the side of the road
to observe the sublime cloud of smoke that emerges when farmers burn off the stubble from their
fields. While this sight is itself incredible, something even more magnificent comes into view: "a

---

[129] *Supra* note 19 at 86-87.
[130] Nicol, *supra* note 6 at 6.
[131] Lainsbury, *supra* note 12 at 236.
[132] *Ibid.*
[133] *Supra* note 27 at 22.

cocaine white egret, a bird [Andy] had never seen in real life before, had flown from the west."[134]
When Andy realizes the bird's proximity to him, he admits to feeling "chosen," and when the
bird swoops directly over him, scraping his scalp in the process, he falls "to his knees," in a
pseudo-religious gesture that outlines the significance of the moment.[135] While in this position,
Andy finds himself "dog-piled by an instant family," which consists of the mentally-challenged
teenagers.[136] Rather than recoiling from such an overt display of emotion, he revels in "their
adoring, healing uncritical embrace . . . They began to hug me – too hard - . . . this *pain* I was
experiencing was no problem at all, in fact, this crush of love was unlike anything I had ever
known."[137] Certainly, such demonstrativeness is quite unlike anything he has ever known while
steeped in the irony he spends the bulk of the novel trying to escape. Perhaps this moment, which
Tate characterizes as an "image of baptism," signifies his victory.[138]

Daniel Grassian offers a less optimistic interpretation of this novel's ending. Suggesting
that the way in which Andy welcomes this "crush of love" underscores the extent to which he
has been deprived of such raw, untainted emotion, Grassian claims this final scene "points out an
important loss of primal emotional connection in postmodern/popular culture."[139] In terms of the
protagonists' mission to substitute sincerity for irony, that "the only people who appear
emotionally healthy in Coupland's *Generation X* are the mentally disabled teenagers" is
discomfiting because they represent the few who remain "presumably untainted."[140] It may be a
crass juxtaposition, but suggesting that one's mental faculties must be deficient in order to be
truly sincere in the era of late capitalism is a rather ominous suggestion with which to end the
novel.

Nevertheless, the final pages of the novel during which this incident is described are
devoid of any slogans or definitions, thus suggesting that it is, to a certain extent, irony-free:
there are no wry definitions that compromise Andy's induction into this powerful emotional
realm. That Andy has this experience near the border of Mexico, a country whose role in the
development of late capitalism is much less conspicuous than that of the United States, raises the
question as to whether the protagonists' original destination, despite its marginality, was still too

---

[134] *Supra* note 44 at 177.
[135] *Ibid*. at 178.
[136] *Ibid*. at 179.
[137] *Ibid*.
[138] *Supra* note 2 at 327.
[139] *Supra* note 41 at 94.
[140] *Ibid*.

close to consumer culture for their desert detox to be entirely successful. In terms of Coupland's larger fictional project, however, what is important is that they made an attempt, however naïve.

Despite the ironic structure of *Generation X*, it is not fair to say that Coupland ultimately capitulates to the prevalence of such wryness. Instead, he toys with it. While the protagonists' anti-commercial objectives are undermined by the definitions that decorate the margins, Coupland ironizes his irony vis-à-vis the pseudo- slogans that appear alongside the definitions. Offering such messages such as "LESS IS A POSSIBILITY" and, "YOU MIGHT NOT COUNT IN THE NEW ORDER," by creating slogans that are actually true because they accurately reflect the protagonists' experience, Coupland is undercutting advertising, a discourse that contributes heavily to the postmodern irony his narrative attempts to combat.[141] Advertising, which is designed to sell products, is out of sync with the economically disadvantaged position of members of Generation X who are unable to purchase what is being pitched. Thus, in a parodic gesture, Coupland includes ad hoc advertising that actually *does* speak to its target market. Coupland's editor referred to these tidbits as "thought-bombs," an appropriate characterization given their aim of exploding the mendacity of advertising.[142]

There are many more side-bar definitions in *Generation X* than the space allotted for this chapter permits me to discuss. Consequently, in the chapters that follow, I will demonstrate that they also provide applicable conceptual frameworks for themes that Coupland explores in *Shampoo Planet, Microserfs,* and *Girlfriend in a Coma,* reinforcing my argument that all four novels treated in this thesis deal with different aspects of Generation X.

---

[141] *Supra* note 44 at 112, 159.
[142] Annsley, *supra* note 31 at 125.

Chapter 2 – Get a Haircut, and Get a Real Job: *Shampoo Planet* and the Expansion of Generation X

Shampoo Planet is a novel that depicts irony more explicitly than it denigrates it. At first glance then, the sarcasm that abounds *Shampoo Planet* suggests it is a novel that veers off course in terms of Coupland's overall literary objective to repudiate postmodern irony. However, this blip in Coupland's novelistic trajectory is explainable because *Shampoo Planet*, by providing a discursive space in which irony mainly flourishes, allows for a more thorough characterization of it. Because irony was under siege in *Generation X*, it was merely referred to rather than depicted at length. *Shampoo Planet*, on the other hand, demonstrates the prevalence of irony and how it actually operates in the late capitalist era. Although Andy, Claire and, Dag provide a more overt rejection of irony, Tyler is by no means a character who fully capitulates to it. Consequently, like *Generation X*, *Shampoo Planet* underscores the importance of genuine communication, a mode of expression that stands in direct opposition to postmodern irony.

The purpose of this chapter is therefore twofold. First I will demonstrate that in spite of how much of the critical commentary that exists on *Shampoo Planet* exploits it as a work that depicts the generation after Generation X, like Coupland's debut novel of the same name, it is really a novel about this demographic in particular, just a different segment of it. Second, it will expand upon the discussion about postmodern irony outlined in the first chapter by providing more explicit examples of the ironic worldview *Generation X* tries to resist. *Shampoo Planet*, like *Generation X*, problematizes this irony, just on a smaller scale. It also revisits various scenes in *Generation X* in order to provide an ironic inversion so that similar circumstances are interpreted through Tyler's perspective rather than that of Andy, Dag, and Claire.

"Yuppie Wannabes": Expanding Generation X

The namesake of *Shampoo Planet*'s protagonist, Tyler, appeared in a different guise in *Generation X* as Andy's younger brother. Coupland "began writing *Shampoo Planet* in order to expand" on this particular character, and, in this novel he gives Tyler the discursive space he deserves.[143] While unlike Andy, Claire, and Dag, Tyler embraces consumer culture and its concomitant irony and firmly believes that his future is bright and bursting with job prospects,

---

[143] Dreher, Rod. "Teenagers Go Global in Coupland's *Shampoo Planet*." *The Washington Times* 17 Sept. 1992. D8.

such tendencies do not disqualify him as a fully-fledged member of Generation X. Despite his grandiose dreams of becoming a corporate high-flyer, Tyler shares two very important similarities with his jaded cohorts: a palpable hostility for the baby boom generation, and the inheritance of a commodified language rife with allusions to pop culture and advertising. Whereas Andy, Dag, and Claire revile this tainted idiom, which is laden with the irony they are so keen to combat, for most of *Shampoo Planet*, Tyler is quite comfortable with it.

The media predominately portrayed Generation X as a group of apathetic "slackers" whose worldview is characterized by "indifference."[144] While Coupland's earnest protagonists in *Generation X* provide a subtle critique of such a narrow conceptualization, the character of Tyler, who subscribes to both *Young Achiever* and *Entrepreneur* magazine, confronts this stereotype head on.[145] There were 41 million GenXers born during the fabled 15-year period of 1965-1980: that every single one of them rejected consumer culture and gave up on having a rewarding and lucrative career and is highly unlikely.[146] Nevertheless, Dreher, like many reviewers, maintains that in *Shampoo Planet*, Coupland portrays "the generation after X" rather than a different subset of Generation X.[147] Statistically, Tyler falls within Generation X territory because he was ten years old "shortly after John Lennon was assassinated," which places his time of birth somewhere around 1970.[148] While *Generation X*, to a certain extent, exemplifies the mainstream perception which posits that generation as group as a bunch of underemployed non-conformists, *Shampoo Planet* gives voice to another constituency of this generation. Coupland briefly, though sardonically, alludes to the existence of this subgroup in *Generation X*: "YUPPIE-WANNABE'S: An *X* generation subgroup that believes the myth of a yuppie life-style being both satisfying and viable."[149] Although Tyler certainly fits this description, such allegiance does not compromise his status as a member of Generation X.

I Shop Therefore I Am: Consumerism as Defense Mechanism

The language used in *Shampoo Planet* often imitates that used in advertising. Coupland's employment of such an idiom is not surprising given Baudrillard's declaration that in

---

[144] Annsley, *supra* note 31 at 3.
[145] Coupland, *Shampoo Planet*, New York: Simon & Schuster, 1992 at 25.
[146] Gowen, Anne. "Coupland's Coup at Embassy." *The Washington Times* 24 Feb. 1994. C10.
[147] *Ibid.*
[148] *Supra* note 145 at 30.
[149] *Supra* note 44 at 91.

contemporary society, "advertising has imposed itself and developed at the expense of all other languages."[150] For example, Tyler, who is obsessed with hair care, sounds more like a commercial than an adolescent when he explains this preoccupation of his:

> Your hair is you . . . What's on top of your head says what's inside your
> head. Wash every day? Use ComPulson®, with marigold and beer.
> Hormone-hair changing texture every five minutes? Use MOODSWING®
> the revitalizing power toner from Sweden with walnut leaf for self-
> damaging hair.[151]

This pontification of his ironically recalls the *Generation X* dictum "Shopping Is Not Creating," because, as far as Tyler is concerned, his hairstyle and hair care regimen form a central, albeit purchased, part of his being.

Unlike the characters of *Generation X* who greet the future with pessimism and disdain, and despite those in *Shampoo Planet* who lose their jobs due to an economic recession, Tyler pays lip service to "the sparkling and thrilling future that [he] desperately want[s] to share."[152] However, such consumer confidence on Tyler's part actually serves to mask his latent insecurities about the future, fears he assuages mainly by shopping, but fears that nonetheless align him with Generation X.

Tyler proclaims he is not worried about falling prey to the recession currently affecting Lancaster, his hometown: "Me, I'll escape. I know that. I have a plan . . . I have a good car and a wide assortment of excellent hair-care products. I know what I want from life; I have ambition."[153] Tyler's belief that that his car and toiletries will protect him from hardship is what Mueke calls "heavy irony" because the incongruity between the statement and the situation is apparent: despite Tyler's faith in consumer products, they will not exempt him from future economic hardship: they are a marketing ploy, not a guarantee.[154] The philosophy that underpins Tyler's consumer habits is defensive shopping: clinging to a media-induced notion of success, he buys into this image by surrounding himself with products that support such an image. Ultimately, shopping gets inserted into a (logically fallacious) late capitalist syllogism: "I want to

---

[150] *Supra* note 112 at 88.
[151] *Supra* note 45 at 7-8.
[152] *Ibid.* at 11.
[153] *Ibid.* at 13.
[154] *Supra* note 52 at 54.

be successful, therefore, I will buy the things I associate with success. Thus, there is no way I will not be successful." Such an attitude has latent implications for Tyler's espousal of the American Dream grand narrative, despite that narrative's lack of viability for members of Generation X, discussed in the previous chapter. While Tyler's professional ambitions suggest that he believes in the American Dream framework, his consumerist philosophy demonstrates that it is a grand narrative he, quite literally, buys into.

Tyler's ambition is channeled towards a prestigious job at Bechtol, a multi-national corporation located in Seattle. His mother is dismayed by his choice because in her youth, she and her friends, during the height of the hippie movement, "used to *firebomb* Bechtol."[155] His response to her criticisms is "Get modern, Jasmine. Bechtol is a fine company in the growth mode and they offer fast advancement potential and a shockingly good pension."[156] Beneath this pension poster-boy, however, Tyler's admonishment to "Get modern," reflects his demographic position, and by extension, perceived downward mobility, as a member of Generation X. Tyler insists that he has to "think ahead" as he tells his mother, "the world was a much better place than when [she was] young," a statement with which Jasmine does not argue because she knows growing up a baby boomer was much easier than growing up as a member of Generation X.[157]

Shampoo Planet plays with the tried-and-true baby boomer/GenXer binary opposition depicted in *Generation X*. Whereas Andy's mother epitomizes the insensitive baby boomer, Jasmine is very unlike Mrs. Palmer because, having been heavily involved with the hippie movement, she does not pose as a poor woman who is really financially secure. Rather, she barely makes enough to support her family through her position as an entry-level data clerk, which could easily qualify as a McJob. It is her parents, much like the loathed bumper-sticker-buying grandparents in *Generation X*, who fill the archetypal shoes of the noxious baby boomer in this novel. As Tyler says,

> I wish I liked Grandpa more than I actually do . . . but . . . after he retired a
> few years ago, it became increasingly apparent that all he was concerned
> with was monitoring his investments, crowing over their success, and
> conspicuously not sharing his winnings with his family.[158]

---

[155] *Supra* note 145 at 16.
[156] *Ibid.*
[157] *Ibid.* at 17.
[158] *Ibid.* at 61.

Comments like this demonstrate that Tyler, like Andy, Claire, and Dag, suffers from "Boomer Envy," not surprising considering his grandfather seems like the type of man whose car would be decorated with a tacky bumper sticker. Sounding more like a GenXer than a future corporate drone, Tyler declares that "young people are doomed" because "Grandma and Grandpa own and run everything."[159] Throughout the novel he insists that "the system is absolutely rigged in their favor."[160]

Nevertheless, Tyler holds fast to his determination and his belief in the American Dream. Anxiety about the veracity of the American Dream, however, is voiced in the novel by Stephanie, Tyler's Parisian love interest, who, because she is not American, is not susceptible to the tenacious mythology of this grand narrative: "Which is more fair: to promise your children the moon and then give your children nothing – or promise only a little – be realistic – so when your children become civil servants or drive a truck they are not unhappy?"[161] She labels the elusive promise of the American Dream as "crool-el" (200). Such an idea of lowered expectation is much more commonly expressed in *Generation X* through the philosophy of "Lessness."[162]

When told by his down-and-out stepfather that he should "just lower [his] expectations," Tyler, however, unlike his *Generation X* counterparts, refuses to accede to such philosophy: "Don't they understand that asking me to lower my expectations is like asking me to change the color of my eyes?"[163] Whereas Andy, Claire, and, to a certain extent, Dag accept a demographically-enforced poverty, Tyler sees poverty as "a wolf baying and clawing at my door, strip by strip, inching that much closer to me."[164] Tyler's fear of poverty is so poignant that when "a vaguely Third World image" appears on his TV screen he "promptly zap[s] to something else."[165] As a way to cope with his fear of poverty, he detaches himself from the possibility of being poor by creating a slogan, "Think poor; be poor," a line of thought that ties in well with his defensive shopping.[166] Tyler, of course, "thinks rich" in an effort to secure himself that ever-

---

[159] *Ibid.* at 80.
[160] *Ibid.* at 293.
[161] *Ibid.* at 222.
[162] The term "Lessness," defined and discussed in the previous chapter, refers to "a philosophy whereby one reconciles oneself with diminishing expectations of material wealth" (*Generation X, supra* note 44 at 54).
[163] *Supra* note 145 at 180.
[164] *Ibid.* at 27.
[165] *Ibid.*
[166] *Ibid.*

elusive corner office in the sky and he "buys rich" as well by only purchasing heavily-advertised, brand name products because anything else is "suspect."[167]

Tyler often envisions his successful future in an effort to help convince himself of its viability. A litany he often repeats while indulging in such visualization is: "I am thinking about the future. I am optimistic about the future. The future to me is like the Bechtol headquarters in Seattle, a shiny black needle, a tall thin building that can deliver a promise – a vaccine."[168] His use of the term vaccine implies that there is something toxic, or diseased about the society in which he currently lives. Such an implication recalls the "desert detox" that Andy, Claire, and Dag undergo. Tyler also trusts that narrative will act as a healing salve, only his chosen story is, ironically, *Life at the Top,* the biography Mr. Frank E. Miller the CEO of Bechtol. Like the "bedtime stories" of *Generation X*, this book, which he has "reread many times" and "heartily recommends" provides a more tangible plot to which Tyler aspires.[169]

However, beneath Tyler's career ambitions lurks serious doubt about his future prospects and the situation of Dan, his step-father, epitomizes of all his fears: "Driving home I pass Dan's soon-to-be-vacated apartment . . . Is Dan what I am slated to become? Him? Scary. Don't *I* have any say in the matter?"[170] That he doubts how much he can really control his future not only calls into question the sincerity of his earlier, more confident statements about his career, but it also reasserts his demographic vulnerability as a member Generation X.

Digging for History: Ironically Rethinking the Vietnam War Memorial

Tyler's proclamation that "TV is here for ten thousand years . . . It will never leave," speaks to how television has emerged as the most prominent medium in today's world.[171] Consequently, formats employed in the televisual realm have had a palpable influence on how people speak and perceive their everyday environment, a tendency that Tyler exemplifies. When asking his mother to elaborate on an idea she brings up during a conversation, he says "please tell the studio audience," demonstrating how he has internalized a communication model commonly used on talk television.[172] He envisions their entire conversation as a broadcasted

---

[167] *Ibid.* at 24.
[168] *Ibid.* at 55.
[169] *Ibid.*
[170] *Ibid.* at 126.
[171] *Ibid.* at 194.
[172] *Ibid.* at 17.

interview rather than an intimate exchange: "Jasmine sits perpendicular to me in the classic talk-show host/side-kick configuration."[173]

The topic of their "show" is Jasmine's anxiety about her daughter's fabricated relationship to history. This discussion about the commodification of history in the contemporary realm ironically revisits a theme introduced in *Generation X*. Jasmine is concerned that Daisy is too focused on the sixties rather than on the present: "I think Daiz is going too far with the sixties thing. I mean, doesn't she want to have a *now*?"[174] Tyler's response reveals his lack of concern and refusal to acknowledge this trend: "They're the McDead, Jasmine. The sixties are like a theme park to them. They wear the costume, buy their ticket and have the experience. Their hair may be long, but it smells great."[175] That Tyler labels his history-consuming sibling as part of the "McDead" movement resonates strongly with Ryan Moore's discussion about the a new, fabricated approach to history, where attending a Grateful Dead concert, once an authentically rebellious gesture, now signifies "a commodified simulacrum pure and simple . . . for at least a day, otherwise well-groomed kids born in the 1970's can put on their tie-dyed tee shirts and 'feel like one of those sixties photographs.'"[176]

In *Generation X*, Andy laments how history has turned into "a press release, a marketing strategy."[177] Ironically, in *Shampoo Planet*, Tyler actually does turn history into a marketing strategy, and he does so on purpose. It is worth noting that in *Generation X* while Andy is pontificating on his conflicted relationship with history, his younger brother Tyler, the namesake and precursor to *Shampoo Planet's* protagonist who accompanies him to the Vietnam War Memorial, is unable to grasp his consternation.[178]

Tyler's characterization of the sixties as a "theme park" in the conversation he has with Jasmine resonates with the project he pitches in a letter to Frank E Miller in which he outlines a winning idea for a historical theme park called "*History World*™":

> our country is having a shortage of historical objects – there are not
> enough old things for people to own. As well, we have too many landfills,
> plus an ever-looming fuel shortage. So, I therefore say, Mr. Miller, "*Why*

---

[173] *Ibid*. at 24.
[174] *Ibid*.
[175] *Ibid*. at 25.
[176] *Supra* note 13 at 257.
[177] *Supra* note 44 at 151.
[178] *Ibid*.

*not combine these three factors with our country's love of theme parks and
come out a winner?"*[179]

He goes on to suggest that people dig through history, as it decomposes in the form of garbage,
because, in today's commodified world, digging through the mud in this way is as close as one
can get to history that is not problematically mediated by the media. That people pay for the
items they recover while scavenging, demonstrates how history is literally something to be
consumed. *Shampoo Planet* thus provides a more satirical commentary on how history is
consumed in a late capitalist society, as this scene differs greatly from Andy's display of angered
nostalgia at the Vietnam War Memorial.

So pervasive are manufactured substances and experiences in the lives of these characters
that Tyler and his girlfriend, while on a road trip to Los Angeles, a city notorious for its
artificiality, create a "list of the chemicals needed In order to be a "truly modern person":
'Tetracycline,' 'Steroids,' 'Freon,' 'Aspartame,' 'Peroxide,' 'Silicon,' 'MTV.'"[180] Their
inclusion of MTV in the list of essential chemicals is telling because it speaks to the
manufactured nature of this channel, as well as its implicit toxicity. Katie Mills describes MTV
as "the single most important force shaping what would come to be called Generation X."[181] That
Tyler considers it a potentially dangerous compound suggests MTV's prominent role in the
dissemination of American pop culture could ultimately be hazardous as well. Its ubiquity,
however, makes it a difficult substance to avoid.

Keep the Platitudes Coming: Telethons as Ironic Signifier

Like the protagonists of *Generation X*, Tyler and Anna-Louise are guarded about
expressing their emotions, lest they appear too sentimental or cheesy. Claire, Andy, and Dag,
when faced with the beauty of the sunrise resort to silence rather than running the risk of
sounding trite. However, Anna-Louise and Tyler embrace the irony and outwardly mock their
corniness by speaking in "telethon-ese," a notoriously platitudinous way of communicating that
demonstrates the impossibility of sincerity in a postmodern era:

---

[179] *Supra* note 145 at 199-200.
[180] *Ibid*. at 199.
[181] *Supra* note 35 at 227.

You're beautiful Tyler". "No *you're* beautiful Anna-Louise". "Tyler, you
are fabulous. Truly fabulous. Stop being so fabulous. Just *stop* it". "I love
you Anna-Louise. From the bottom of my heart" "Anna-Lousie, the work
you do for those kids. It's [. . .] *beautiful*." "Let's hear those phones start
to ring.[182]

Their hackneyed conversation epitomizes Umberto Eco's notion of postmodern irony, a
condition which he describes as "that of a man who loves . . . a very cultivated woman and
knows he cannot say to her, 'I love you madly,' because he knows that she knows that these
words have already been written" and thus will seem fatuous.[183] Accordingly, Tyler explains that
"If Anna-Louise and I make too big a deal about liking each other, we feel corny," so they must
resort to couching their sentiments in irony.[184]

Corresponding with Eco's notion of commodified language is Coupland's concept of
"O'PROPRIATION," which he introduces in *Generation X* and defines as "The inclusion of
advertising, packaging and entertainment jargon from earlier eras in everyday speech for ironic
and/or comic effect."[185] Douglas Rushkoff argues that this strategy of ironic distancing
epitomizes GenX consciousness: "The moment GenX began was the moment when the first
buster 'bracketed' his own experience, the minute someone stepped back and, in a wink-wink-
say-no-more fashion, related the ironic distance he felt from his own experience."[186] While this
distance is problematized by Andy, Claire, and Dag, who try to close the gap by resisting
consumer culture, which is the main cause of commodified language, the characters in *Shampoo
Planet* depict this distance in all its alienating splendor.

When Tyler refers to his friends' tired prattle as a "maxed-out credit card," his use of this
simile demonstrates the extent to which language has been completely used up and drained of its
significance.[187] Such a characterization has inauspicious implications about the quality of
communication in contemporary society because it suggests we have reached our loquacious

---

[182] *Supra* note 145 at 28.
[183] *Supra* note 34 at 111.
[184] *Supra* note 145 at 35.
[185] *Supra* note 44 at 107.
[186] *Supra* note 18 at 10.
[187] *Supra* note 145 at 53.

limit: there is no room left for original expression as the sincerity of language has been maximized, or reached its proverbial credit limit.

Say It With Flowers: The Struggle for Sincerity in *Shampoo Planet*

Beneath his wry, ironic exterior, Tyler has a sentimental side which, like the protagonists of *Generation X*, he is apprehensive about displaying. When expressing his appreciation for flowers, he beseeches the reader to "bear with [his] corniness."[188] Once he has provided this affective disclaimer, he explains,

> I believe that what you do with flowers reveals what you do with your
> love . . . Last week I bought a box of 250 crocus bulbs and planted them in
> the dirt outside of Anna-Louise's bedroom window, arranged so that after
> blooming in April they will spell the words LOVE ME.[189]

Though his horticultural gesture is certainly a more genuine expression of love than his impression of a telethon host, he is still unable to express thoughts of this sentimental magnitude verbally, a difficulty he eventually begins to overcome by the novel's ending.

He is similarly reticent to share his true thoughts with his friend Harmony, who asks him what he thinks would be the "coolest way to die."[190] Tyler has two responses to this question: the one he shares, and the one he would like to share, but does not:

> Before I reflexively blurted out a stock response like "naked in a car crash
> with the tuneage cranked to eleven," I paused and thought of a person like
> me, growing up in a flower-free part of the world . . . and admiring an
> acid-yellow field of zinnias. Suddenly *whoosh!* Along comes a blast of
> Pacific wind, rousing the zinnias into a pollen fervor and blasting me with
> yellowness, shake-and-baking me with a substance I had no idea I was
> allergic to, and within moments, I go into anaphylactic shock and am
> dead. "I don't know Harmony. Naked in a car crash, I guess. With the
> tuneage cranked to eleven."[191]

---

[188] *Ibid*. at 136.
[189] *Ibid*. at 136-37.
[190] *Ibid*. at 138.
[191] *Ibid*.

His answer to this question ultimately reveals that these "stock" responses are safer, because they save him from undergoing the risks involved with describing a situation that is not commonly depicted in an action movie or performed by a stunt driver in an automobile commercial. That his fantasy involves flowers is significant because his fear of being perceived as corny by Harmony recalls the similar trepidation he expressed before expressing before describing his feelings for Anna Louise.

Early in the novel, sensitivity is not Tyler's strong suit. When confronted with the potentially emotionally wrenching discovery that Jasmine and Dan are getting a divorce, rather than respond with despair Tyler describes how "panic washes over [him]" because he wonders whether the divorce will affect his "credit rating."[192] He is not so much concerned with how his parents' separation will affect his social status, such as whether he will be saddled with pernicious social labels such as "child of a broken home," but rather how the collapse of his parents' marriage will adversely impact his purchasing power. That is to say, his immediate response is to consider the economic, rather than the emotional, implications of the situation.

Hollywood Squares, or, The Evolution of Success in *Shampoo Planet*

Despite his steadfast belief in the redeeming power of Bechtol and the American Dream, when Tyler moves to California in order to pursue his career, his expectations are not met. Consequently, in true GenXer fashion, he takes on his first McJob.[193] However, unlike Andy, Dag and Claire who accept McJobs as part of "Lessness," and hold such positions until the very end of the novel, Tyler becomes frustrated with being an economic prisoner after merely a few weeks:

> I quit my job at WingWorld yesterday. I decided I will not burn wings
> every day merely to give myself enough sustenance to be able to continue
> working at WingWorld to make enough sustenance to continue working at
> WingWorld to . . . the loop of evil. Who invented these McJobs, anyway?
> They're work, but they're not a living. The undead working at unlabor.[194]

---

[192] *Ibid*. at 49.
[193] *Ibid*. at 177.
[194] *Ibid*. at 252.

The quitting of McJobs, however, is where the similarity to *Generation X* ends and the irony begins. While Andy, Claire and Dag quit in order to pursue their low-key lifestyle in Mexico because they, perhaps naively, see this destination as a pristine environment devoid of commercial contamination, Tyler seeks solace in Hollywood, where he parlays the cultural obsession with celebrities into his escape from the drudgery of menial labour. Indeed, the "seriously scorching entrepreneurial idea" that enables him to quit his McJob involves profiting from the ultimate from of consumption considered loathsome in *Generation X*: tourism in the form of "purchased experiences." Tweaking his earlier notion of "history as theme park," Tyler enables consumers to "buy" their own simulated piece of history by producing cheaply-made crayon rubbings of the stars on Hollywood Boulevard.

"Life at the Top": Tyler's Emotional, and Professional, Progress

In another ironic revisiting of *Generation X*, in *Shampoo Planet*, Coupland portrays the accursed "veal-fattening pens," so vituperatively loathed by Dag, from Tyler's exalting perspective. When he tours Bechtol for the first time before undergoing his job interview, he revels in, rather than recoils from, the office environment:

> We stroll through a maze of offices: low-eyestrain gray-and-emerald paint
> and carpet; plush sound baffles; glass walls surrounding mini-conference
> rooms; a digital chart monitoring Bechtol's New York Stock Exchange
> performance; unplugged computers dreaming of pie charts; ample aisle
> space for smooth traffic flow; multiple keypad and voiceprint
> identification barriers. The office is all too much for me.[195]

By the end of the novel, against all demographic odds, Tyler is offered the corporate position at Bechtol he dreams of , and his vision of the American Dream comes true: "Two weeks from now I will move to Seattle to join the hospitality-quality-control division of Bechtol's Pacific Northwest Region. I'll have a company car, medical/dental, training seminars, and productivity bonuses."[196]

---

[195] *Ibid*. at 271.
[196] *Ibid*. at 273.

However, his employment contract is not the culmination of his development as an individual. On his way home from the interview, Tyler has an emotional breakthrough similar to those experienced by Andy, Claire, and Dag, though, in another reversal, his epiphany is spurred by success, rather than failure:

> The old woman sitting across the aisle from me falls asleep and her
> dentures fall into her lap then onto the floor. I pick them up and put them
> in her hands, pulling her fingers across them so that they won't slip out
> again. I the return to my seat and something happens to me – something
> inside me is exhausted and worn out and stops spinning and I break down
> and cry. I cry because the future has once again found its sparkle and has
> grown a million times larger. And I cry because I am ashamed of how
> badly I behaved during my own personal Dark Ages.[197]

This sentimental outpouring is rather unexpected from the character that throughout the bulk of the novel is quite solipsistic and sarcastic and speaks like a Public Relations executive on a spinning streak rather than a young adult. However, that he characterizes his former, detached behaviour as his "personal Dark Ages" signifies his realization that the ironic armour he adopted was a primitive defense against alienation, and one that must be improved upon. Like the characters of *Generation X*, Tyler holds himself emotionally rigid. His wall does come down though, and symbolically, at this point in the novel, his "hair is loose, uncombed – kind of just happening all by itself. A first for me. I'm trying to change."[198] He promises to try harder to "Make myself vulnerable," and he does so by attempting to genuinely express his feelings for Anna Louise.[199] When he addresses her in the final pages of the novel, he does not need any affective disclaimer or rely upon the ironic distance of telethon-ese. Instead, he earnestly tells her that when he first met her she smelled of all "the countries I always wanted to visit but never thought I'd be able to. It was like you had the world inside you."[200] To Tyler, and to Anna Louise, such sentiments no longer seem mawkish; they have become meaningful.

---

[197] *Ibid.* at 274.
[198] *Ibid.* at 278.
[199] *Ibid.*
[200] *Ibid.* at 277.

Whereas *Generation X* relegated irony to the margins, *Shampoo Planet* incorporates it into its actual pages as the novel provides a thorough overview of the various guises of postmodern irony. While both novels challenge this irony, *Shampoo Planet* is much more subtle in its repudiation. While Tyler copes with the same affective disorder as Andy, Claire, and Dag, *Shampoo Planet* is a novel that focuses on diagnosing the symptoms of irony rather than attempting to cure them. Thus, *Shampoo Planet* allows for a more comprehensive understanding of the sources, and the pervasiveness, of the irony pathologized in *Generation X*. One key way in which Coupland accomplishes this objective is by inverting or revisiting themes and scenes from *Generation X* so that they can be filtered through Tyler's lens. So, while both *Generation X* and *Shampoo Planet* depict the challenge of affectivity members of Generation X face due to the fact that their formative years coincide with the emergence of late capitalism, each is a work that depicts these generation-specific issues from different viewpoints, hence demonstrating Coupland's sensitivity to the heterogeneity of this demographic.

Chapter 3 – Generation X at Work: *Microserfs* and the Importance of Being 1.0

In many ways, *Microserfs* is a rewriting of *Generation X*, only, like *Shampoo Planet*, it is a narrative told from the perspective of a different segment of this demographic: that of the Microserfs. Also known as also known as Daniel, Susan, Karla, Abe, Michael, Bug, and Todd, these characters all hold jobs as software testers at Microsoft. Although they are well remunerated, the title of this novel aptly describes the servile role the Microserfs play in this corporation's chain of command. While the Microserfs do not have to contend with the grueling humiliation often associated with underemployment, their dissatisfaction with their positions at Microsoft inspires them to embark upon a journey similar to that of Andy, Claire, and Dag. Whereas the protagonists in *Generation X* feel alienated by a society whose preoccupation with consumer culture they do not share, the Microserfs feel alienated as a result of the nature of the work they do for Microsoft. An examination of their undesirable working conditions uncovers the alienation that results from their position as software serfs, and in so doing, offers another angle on Generation X's relationship to irony: that which results from the dehumanizing detachment of the corporate workspace. At Microsoft, efficiency and productivity is revered above all else. So influential is this paradigm that the Microserfs begin striving for it outside the workplace, and consequently begin to resemble the very computers they work with.

This chapter establishes how their desire to transcend the punishing corporate practices of Microsoft is analogous to their deeper desire to unburden themselves from the alienation and detachment that corrodes their world view. In this regard, *Microserfs* differs in a significant way from *Generation X* because the characters try to escape the ironic detachment that their jobs at Microsoft necessarily entail in favour of more autonomous and creative work. This time, however, their endeavour, which is similar to Andy, Claire, and Dag's journey to the desert, is not ironized by Coupland. In fact, once the Microserfs begin work at *Oop!*, a software firm one of them founds, any sense of ironic detachment evaporates from the novel, and is replaced with the characters' attempt to find meaning and happiness in their lives. Therefore, in *Microserfs*, Coupland leaves the structural irony that framed *Generation X* behind, and moves one step closer to the explicit renunciation of irony he undertakes in *Girlfriend in a Coma*.

David Segal muses about the disparate linguistic registers invoked throughout the novel's development, suggesting that "one moment it's a sitcom with glib banter and laugh tracks; then suddenly it has the leaden pathos of a made-for-TV disease movie."[201] As discussed in the introduction to this book, McInerney characterizes these competing tendencies as Coupland's "dual authorial personalities," and it is precisely this "split narrative personality" that enables Coupland to depict the ironic woes associated with Generation X's late capitalist existence only to problematize, and eventually renounce, this irony.[202] *Microserfs* provides the most balanced example of Coupland's mission because while all the novels discussed in this book feature an ideological battle between irony and sentimentality, it organizes these competing poles into a cohesive and complete narrative in which irony is depicted and then disavowed. In the first chapter, I argued that *Generation X* functions as a novelistic "after photo" in that it depicts characters who have already decided to alter their lifestyle in order to escape the trappings of a consumer society. The second chapter then demonstrated how *Shampoo Planet*, while thematically similar to *Generation X*, functions as a "before photo" because it provides a detailed representation of the irony problematized in *Generation X*. *Microserfs*, however, provides the complete picture as it depicts the before, during, and after phases of the characters' journey away from the ironic detachment that is part of Microsoft's corporate landscape.

Bottomed-Out Boomers: Inverting the Demographics of Generation X

While *Shampoo Planet* exemplifies, yet also expands, the traditional Generation X/Baby Boomer dichotomy put forth in *Generation X*, *Microserfs* pushes this issue one step further by framing GenXers as the ones at an advantage rather than a disadvantage. Demographically, the Microserfs are members of Generation X because the novel, written in diary entry format, begins in 1993. Therefore, Daniel, aged 26, would have been born in 1967, statistically making him a member of Generation X, along with his friends who are roughly the same age. *Microserfs* then, like *Shampoo Planet*, demonstrates how Coupland further expands the conventional characterization of the Generation X/Baby Boomer binary by inverting it, hence offering a different take on this often misunderstood demographic.

---

[201] Segal, David. "An Empty Tale of Modern Times." *The Washington Post* 13 Jul. 1995: 1-2. *Lexus-Nexus.* InfoTrac. MacLennan Library, McGill University, Montreal, QC. 01 Nov. 2004.
[202] *Supra* note 14 at 1.

Although Daniel is merely a coder at Microsoft, thus relatively low on the proverbial totem pole, his father, who has worked in management at IBM throughout most of his career, is the one who loses his job: "Dad got fired! Didn't we see that one coming a mile away. This whole restructuring business."[203] Whereas in *Generation X* it is the demographically disadvantaged twenty-somethings who struggle to find employment, this trend is reversed in *Microserfs* where, due to rapid technological advancements, it is "the fifty-somethings being dumped out of the economy by downsizing."[204] Daniel's father, unable to find a new job, tells his son dejectedly, "it's your world now."[205] Such a statement is a complete reversal of Tyler's assertion in *Shampoo Planet* that the world is "rigged" in favour of the Baby Boomers. In *Microserfs*, the tables really have turned because not only does Daniel send his father 500 dollars every month in order to compensate for his lost income, but also, when he is completely without job prospects, Michael hires him to work at *Oop!* as an adjunct handyman who helps construct their office. Daniel's mother figures her husband is "just caught in this weird demographic glitch," a statement that comes across as somewhat ironic considering in *Shampoo Planet* and *Generation X*, such a characterization applies to members of Generation X rather than the Baby Boomers[206].

However, not all boomers find themselves suddenly unemployed like Mr. Underwood. At Microsoft, there are still palpable inter-generational tensions. Nevertheless, in *Microserfs*, such tension is more aptly labeled as "Boomer Annoyance" rather than the "Boomer Envy" featured in *Generation X* and *Shampoo Planet*. Daniel describes Microsoft as a "status theme park" wherein those higher up on the ladder are usually Baby Boomers in possession of far more stock options.[207] These "set-for-lifers" though are portrayed as irritating, out-of-touch wannabes rather than a repugnant force that robs the younger generation of its future prospects. Shaw, Daniel's supervisor is a "Baby Boomer" and to Daniel's dismay, "he and his ilk are responsible for (let me rant for a second) this thing called 'The Unitape' – an endless loop of elevator jazz Microsoft plays at absolutely every company function."[208] Such condescending qualms, however, seem

---

[203] Douglas Coupland, *Microserfs*. Toronto: HarperCollins, 1995 at 21.
[204] *Ibid.* 23.
[205] *Ibid.* at 41.
[206] *Ibid.* at 279.
[207] *Ibid.* at 9.
[208] *Ibid.* at 33.

rather minor and trivial when compared to the accusations Dag wields against the Boomers in *Generation X*.

There Is a God, Bill Gates Be Thy Name: Microsoft as Pseudo-Religion

Like the protagonists of *Generation X,* the Microserfs feel that they lack a grand narrative that explains and guides their lives. As Daniel explains:

> you have to remember that most of us who've moved to Silicon Valley,
> we don't have the traditional identity-donating structures like other places
> in the world have: religion, politics, cohesive family structure, roots, a
> sense of history or other prescribed self belief systems that take the onus
> off individuals having to figure out who they are.[209]

Instead of establishing a "bedtime story" club like Andy, Claire, and Dag as a way to compensate for such discursive deprivation, the Microserfs superimpose a religious grand narrative on their boss, Bill Gates, the founder of Microsoft. Daniel admits that the deification of Bill Gates is somewhat phony because "if it weren't for the cult of Bill," then Microsoft would be nothing but a "great big office supply company."[210] Nevertheless, his placing Gates on such a pedestal speaks to the need to believe in something, especially when faced with the dismantlement of traditional grand narratives. Daniel suspects as much when he suggests that "maybe this whole Bill thing is actually the subconscious manufacture of God."[211] As a result, before the serfs leave Microsoft, Bill Gates functions as a God in their world which lacks such omniscience. The novel opens with Daniel declaring like a devoted disciple, "Bill is wise. Bill is kind. Bill is benevolent. Bill, Be My Friend . . . *Please!*"[212]

"The cult of Bill" signifies not only the need for a grand narrative, but also the need for an authority who renders important and significant the often intellectually-nullifying work of Microsoft employees who write, test, and debug computer code "one line at a time, one line in a strand of millions."[213] In this sense, Bill Gates acts as an Orwellian presence whose influence stretches beyond the realm of a typical corporate boss: "the presence of Bill floats about the

---

[209] *Ibid*. at 236.
[210] *Ibid*. at 35.
[211] *Ibid*. at 16.
[212] *Ibid*. at 1.
[213] *Ibid*. at 2.

Campus, semi-visible, at all times . . . Bill is a moral force, a spectral force, a force that shapes, a force that molds. A force with thick, thick, glasses."[214] The force that Gates embodies signifies a type of rags-to-riches grand narrative comparable to the American Dream, but combined with a dose of *Revenge of the Nerds*, the 1984 film directed by Jeff Kanew that depicted how marginalized nerds rose to social prominence. Bill Gates not only represents the entrepreneurial acumen associated with the American Dream, but in so doing, he also provides hope for all the once marginalized nerds by making computers, previously relegated to the realm of the geeky, an incredibly influential part of contemporary society. As such, Gates represents not only a successful, though thickly bespectacled, CEO, but he also symbolizes the dominant role that computers have come to play in society in that the "cult of Bill" also involves the worship of computers.

Computers are known for their mechanized efficiency, and by personally exemplifying this trait, Bill makes it a desirable goal towards which his underlings strive. Michael worshipfully describes him as "efficient. People forget that he is medically, biologically, a genius. Not one ummm or ahhh from his mouth . . . no wasted brain energy. Truly an inspiration for us all."[215] Conscious of his own tendency to say "ummmm" too much, Dan is so impressed by Gates's flawless colloquy that he vows to do "a mental Find-and-Replace on [him]self" in an effort to "debug" his speech patterns.[216] Daniel Grassian states that the serfs' proclivity to both "deify" Gates and "describe him as being mechanistic" is a significant coincidence because:

> His power lies in his lack of emotion and his cool robotic method of
> appearing beyond the human world. Gates is not only the serfs' dream of
> success, but he also appears to be their unstated dream of shedding their
> emotions and bodies.[217]

Notably, once Daniel and the rest of the serfs are comfortably established in their own software company, *Oop!*, which they travel to a technology conference in Las Vegas to promote, Gates ceases to have such tenacious power over them. Gates is also at the conference, and when confronted with his presence in this different context, Daniel compares "seeing his face and

---

[214] *Ibid.* at 3.
[215] *Ibid.* at 31.
[216] *Ibid.* at 177.
[217] *Supra* note 41 at 135.

hearing his voice" to "being teleported back to eleventh-grade chem class. Like a distant dream."[218] However, while he no longer holds the elevated status of a deity for Daniel, Bill's influence is still prevalent for others: "people were *riveted* to his every gesture. I mean *riveted*."[219] Reinforcing Grassian's earlier comments, Daniel surmises that people are drawn to Gates because he embodies the "core of the nerd dream" which involves not having "to express emotion or charisma, because emotion can't be converted into lines of code."[220] Daniel, however, is not riveted by Bill's presence anymore. Rather he "kind of lost focus after a while" and continues walking around the convention centre.[221] This renunciation demonstrates that Daniel and the serfs turned have not only their back on Bill, but they have also shrugged off the nerd dream of detachment, an emotional realm ultimately connected to the corporate dominance of Microsoft, but not espoused by their new employer.

Machines with Paycheques, or, Life as a Microserf

Perhaps the most startling aspect of the Microserfs' tenure at Microsoft is how "their incessant work with computers has helped make them increasingly mechanistic."[222] The mechanization of the human body is a trope in *Microserfs* that reflects the alienation that is part of the serfs' experience at Microsoft. Daniel's aforementioned desire to "debug" his speech patterns is one example of many in the novel that demonstrate how, while working at Microsoft, the Microserfs feel and act more like machines than people. Accordingly, when he introduces himself, rather than providing his proper legal name, he says "I'm danielu@microsoft.com," a gesture that exhibits how he identifies more with his email address in which Microsoft literally forms part of his identity.[223] The most poignant example of this identification with computers emerges when Daniel attempts to improve his life as though he were repairing a computer. He feels like "something is missing" and in order to discover just what this is, he undertakes to write a diary, not so much to sort out his feelings, but in order "to try and see the patterns in my life. From this I hope to establish what my problem is – and then, hopefully, solve it."[224] This

---

[218] *Supra* note 203 at 355.
[219] *Ibid.*
[220] *Ibid.*
[221] *Ibid.*
[222] Grassian, *supra* note 41 at 135.
[223] *Supra* note 203 at 67.
[224] *Ibid.* at 4.

approach is similar to what he does on a daily basis when trying to remove the bugs from line after line of computer code.

Michael's comments later in the novel shed light upon what it is Daniel is seeking, as well as the Microserfs' tendency to model themselves after the machines with which they spend the bulk of their time. He tells Daniel that "all these years, I have been subliminally modeling my personality after machines – because machines never have to worry about human things."[225] The self-mechanization that results from his job at Microsoft distances the Microserfs from their human capacity to feel emotions, and it is this unnatural, though purposeful detachment, articulated as the nerd dream, that Daniel laments. Ironically, it is by conceptualizing himself as a computer that he realizes he is not one.

In order to better understand the emotional and mental states of the Microserfs, it is necessary to study them in their natural habitat, which, for them, means at work. Much in the way that late capitalism involves the seeping of capitalist activities into every area of life, the late capitalist workspace involves the expansion of the office in a similar manner. Whereas industrial capitalism is closely associated with the pernicious time clock, which, for all its faults, clarified the boundary between work and home, "in the 1980s, corporate integration punctured the *next* realm of corporate life invasion at 'campuses' like Microsoft and Apple – with the next level of intrusion being that the borderline between work and life blurred to the point of unrecognizability."[226] The replacement of the time clock mentality of industrial capitalism with a ubiquitous workplace is one of the hallmarks of contemporary employment.[227] Graham Thompson describes the recent corporate trend of allowing "employees to move their homes inside their own offices" by supplying kitchens, food, and beverages on site."[228] At Microsoft, Daniel fully avails himself of the "Bill-supplied free beverages," regularly consuming "three diet cokes" or more over the duration of his eighteen-hour shifts.[229] Although the provision of such amenities ostensibly facilitates employees' lives, really, corporations are just making it easier for them to spend more time at the office.

---

[225] *Ibid.* at 183.
[226] Thompson, Graham. "'Frank Lloyd Oop': *Microserfs*, Modern Migration and the Architecture of the Nineties." *Canadian Review of American Studies* 31.3 (2001): 119-35 at 123.
[227] *Ibid.*
[228] *Ibid.*
[229] *Supra* note 203 at 16.

Thompson's research shows that corporations like Microsoft are increasing the services available to employees at work, thus making it less and less necessary to leave the premises:

> at the offices of Netscape a dentist visits several times a week so
> employees don't have to leave work to take care of their teeth; Excite has
> office laundry facilities for workers who don't have the time to do their
> washing at home.[230]

Considering these recent trends, it is no wonder that Daniel declares "I am 26 and my universe consists of home, Microsoft, and Costco."[231] Considering that his dwelling place, his job, and the occasional trip to a shopping centre are the axes of existence in his world, it is little wonder that he feels "something is missing" from his life.[232]

Microserfs as Coupland's Critique of Corporate Culture

Grassian aligns the alienation felt by the Microserfs with a desire on Coupland's part to "criticize the corporate environment of Microsoft and like-minded corporations that exploit their workers.[233] There are two levels on which this exploitation takes place. First, economically, in that the workers are "alienated from the products of their own making, from which their superiors receive great profits, while they, the workers, receive a mere sliver of the economic pie."[234] Second, physically, in that employees are overworked and their sedentary lifestyle alienates them from their own bodies. As a result of endless hours spent hunched over his computer at Microsoft, Daniel's physical activity is severely diminished: "I don't even do many sports anymore and my relationship with my body has gone all weird. I used to play soccer three times a week and now I feel like a boss in charge of an underachiever."[235] Daniel's frustration with his job highlights both the physical and economic aspects of this alienation:

> I got to thinking of my cramped, love-starved, sensationless existence at
> Microsoft – and I got so pissed off. And now I just want to forget the
> whole business and get on with living – with being alive. I want to forget

---

[230] *Supra* note 226 at 126-127.

[231] *Supra* note 203 at 3.

[232] *Ibid.*

[233] *Supra* note 41 at 134.

[234] *Ibid.*

[235] *Supra* note 203 at 4.

> the way my body was ignored, year in, year out, in the pursuit of code, in
> the pursuit of someone *else's* abstraction.[236]

This stark realization that all of his intellectual toil and physical sacrifice is done in "pursuit of someone else's abstraction," or, in order to develop software for a company in whose astronomical profits he will not share despite his labours, is what motivates him to leave Microsoft and accept a position at *Oop!*, Michael's start-up company in California. As Grassian states, at *Oop!*, "for the first time in their lives, they are personally invested in all aspects of their business" so it is their abstraction, or program, that benefits from their hard work, not Bill Gates's.[237]

The isolation the Microserfs endure at work reduces their desire for human contact outside of the office, thus exacerbating their alienation. Daniel lauds email as a mode of communication precisely because it limits the potential for human contact:

> The cool thing with e-mail is that when you send it, there's no possibility
> of connecting with the person on the other end. It's better than phone
> answering machines, because with them, the person on the other line
> might actually pick up the phone and you might have to talk.[238]

In light of the above comments, the format of Daniel's answering machine is quite revealing. Its pseudo-automated nature, which wryly imitates the infuriating automated process used to triage calls placed to customer service lines, demonstrates how technology has created an ethos of detachment wherein human contact is minimized and the recorded voice plays the role of a live person:

> Thank you for phoning the powerful Underwood personal messaging
> center. Press *one* for Broyhill furniture. Press *two* for STP, the racer's
> edge, Press *three* for the roomy, affordable Buick Skylark, Press *four* for
> Rice-A-Roni, the San Francisco treat, Press *five* for the Turtle Wax, Press
> *six* for Dan, Press *pound* to repeat this menu.[239]

---

[236] *Ibid*. at 91.
[237] *Ibid*. at 138.
[238] *Ibid*. at 22.
[239] *Ibid*. at 91.

That Daniel, the only live person available via this menu, is the last option after a series of advertising sound bytes, reveals his internalization of the implicit hierarchy of late capitalism where products come before people. Importantly, before departing for California, Dan erases "the voice mail message that has served me well for the past six months" (91). The erasure of this message signals the beginning of his repudiation of an ironic, detached existence in which advertising is the predominant idiom in exchange for something more genuine.

The antisocial preferences which Daniel explains, notably, at the beginning of the novel are replaced with unmechanized feelings of love as the novel progresses. Demonstrating the beginning of his shift from detachment to attachment, he describes this bond in very sentimental terms, and in a tone that is antithetical to that of his sardonic answering machine message: "And when you meet someone and fall in love, and they fall in love with you, you ask them, 'Will you take my heart – stains and all?' and they say, 'I will,' and they ask you the same question, and you say, 'I will,' too."[240] Throughout the first part of the novel, which is devoted to describing the plight of the alienated Microserfs, Daniel repeatedly states "I really need a life, bad," thus demonstrating his awareness that his current disaffected state is problematic and lacking.[241] As the remainder of *Microserfs* shows, what exactly constitutes "having a life" is a notion closely linked with transcending the dehumanizing side-effects of being a Microsoft employee. Thus, when he victoriously declares, upon falling in love with Karla, that "there is life after not having a life. I never expected love to happen. What *was* I expecting from life, then?" it signals a change in his preference for the dehumanized detachment of in favour of the human connection provided by love.[242]

What Does it Matter? : Irony as Detachment

Microserfs is a novel whose irony is subtle, and is located mostly in actions that symbolize its larger themes. How the Microserfs respond to their "Ship It" awards, which Microsoft employees receive in honour of meeting their product deadlines, underlies the ironic detachment they feel from their work. Rather than treasure these "12 x 15 x 1 inch Lucite slab[s]," in a symbolic gesture that expresses just how apathetic they are towards their jobs, they

---

[240] *Ibid.* at 57.
[241] *Ibid.* at 27.
[242] *Ibid.* at 58.

attempt, unsuccessfully, to destroy these badges of productivity: "Michael has a Ship-It award
and we've tried various times to destroy it – blowtorching, throwing it off the verandah, dowsing
it with acetone to dissolve it."[243] However, to their dismay, these awards are "so permanent, it's
frightening."[244]

The inscription on each plaque reads "EVERY TIME A PRODUCT SHIPS, IT TAKES
US ONE STEP CLOSER TO THE VISION: A COMPUTER ON EVERY DESK AND IN
EVERY HOME."[245] Daniel ironically undermines such a mission when he imagines "some new
species in fifty million years, unearthing one of these profoundly unbiodegradable little gems and
trying to deduce something meaningful about the species and culture that created it."[246] Seriously
calling into question the possibility of extracting a profound message from such a mission
statement, Daniel envisions an exchange that members of this new species have years later upon
discovering a "Ship It" award:

> Surely they lived not for the moment but for some distant time – obviously
> a time far, far beyond their own era, to have created such an astounding
> artifact that would not decay. Yes, Yeltar, and they inscribed profound,
> meaningful and transcendent text inside this miraculously preserved clear
> block, but alas, its message remains forever cryptic.[247]

The inscription is therefore cast in a cynical light when the dubious, blatantly capitalist, and
ultimately alienating mission it describes is seen as "profound, meaningful and transcendent" by
creatures that likely have no idea about the pernicious implications a mission statement
embodies. Consequently, it is symbolic that the Microserfs go to such great lengths to try to
destroy their "Ship It" awards as these destructive gestures signify their disavowal of the values
associated with such an award and the company that promotes them. Of course, by moving to
California and working at a company like *Oop!* they are able to communicate such opposition
much more effectively, just as Dag is better able to address his pent-up aggression during
"bedtime story" hour rather than by vandalizing cars.

---

[243] *Ibid*. at 10.
[244] *Ibid*.
[245] *Ibid*. at 47.
[246] *Ibid*.
[247] *Ibid*.

Immediately after the attempted destruction of the "Ship-It" award, the Microserfs have the crisis of conscience that motivates them to move to Silicon Valley. Considering the complicity of television as a lynchpin of consumer culture, it is not surprising that these anti-capitalist realizations occur when "the Cablevision was out for some reason."[248] Wryly quoting one of Microsoft's corporate objectives, Todd states that "there has to be more to existence than this. *'Dominating as many areas of automated consumerism as possible.'*"[249]

He then continues, bringing assembly-line terminology into the computer age by asking, "Don't you ever feel like a cog, Dan? Wait – the term 'cog' is outdated – a *cross-platform highly transportable binary object*?"[250] Although Daniel responds by telling Todd "work isn't, and was never *meant* to be a person's whole life," his assertion is ironically belied by his earlier statement in which he declares his existence consists of Microsoft, sleep and Costco.[251] Work *does* dominate the lives of the Microserfs, a fact that is quite disconcerting considering how apathetic they are towards their jobs, and how their work results in their resembling the machines used in their jobs. Introspectively, Todd asks, "Where does *morality* enter our lives, Dan? How do we justify what we do to the rest of humanity? Microsoft is no Bosnia."[252] This question reflects a lofty shift in tone from the adolescent males who tried to destroy a "Ship-It" award by strapping it to their car. Nevertheless, it is a question motivated by the same thought process: why do they spend such an enormous amount of time and energy at a company like Microsoft when all they receive for their trouble, besides a paltry paycheque, is a tacky plaque?

Daniel is at first resistant to this foray into the philosophical realm and, in a response heavy with the "knee-jerk irony" introduced in *Generation X,* he snidely attributes Todd's questions to his "religious upbringing."[253] His automatic sarcasm bespeaks a proclivity also displayed in *Generation X* and *Shampoo Planet*: the difficulty of expressing emotional depth in the late capitalist era where sarcasm, rather than sincerity, is instinctive. Whereas the first two novels featured characters who were concerned with appearing trite, *Microserfs* features characters who at first resist considering tough questions about the significance of their work and their lives, but gradually, they learn how to face these issues just like Tyler, Andy, Claire, and

---

[248] *Ibid*. at 60.
[249] *Ibid*.
[250] *Ibid*.
[251] *Ibid*. at 3.
[252] *Ibid*. at 60.
[253] *Ibid*. at 61.

Dag learn how to express emotions. Karla takes the first step towards this type of contemplation when she exclaims that "the *real* morality here, Todd, is whether these good hands are squandered on uncreative lives."[254] And it is the Microserfs decision to leave Microsoft for *Oop!* that protects them from "squandering" their lives in this manner because at Michel's new start-up company, creativity comprises an integral part of their work.

The Symbolism of Software: The Importance of Being 1.0

Because software is "the medium through which human-computer interaction takes place,"[255] the nature of that interaction is of the utmost importance. As the *Oop!* Microsoft binary exemplifies, the way in which software is used can mean the difference between it being a tool that enables its user to be creative or the user becoming a type of mechanized tool himself.[256] As Thompson indicates, the software developed at *Oop!* "stands as a powerful literary metaphor" because it allows its user to play an active role in the realm of creative production.[257]

Computer software serves a metonymic function in *Microserfs* as the office software the serfs debug at Microsoft is juxtaposed with the creative gaming software they create at *Oop!* in order to distinguish between the alienating and empowering functions each product represents as well as the nature of the companies that create them. While Microsoft epitomizes the dehumanizing, all-consuming corporation, *Oop!* represents a workplace that empowers, rather than estranges, its employees.

Microsoft Office is a software suite that emphasizes work rather than personal creativity. Consequently, while at Microsoft, the serfs ironically slave to perfect software that helps people employed at other corporations around the world be more effective, despite the fact that these positions are potentially as alienating as theirs. At *Oop!* Michael thinks he can find a way to make software empowering for those who use it as well as those who design it by transforming the "Object Oriented Programming" platform used for many Microsoft products into a game called "*Oop!*" that allows the user to create rather than merely perform a function.[258] *Oop!* software is described as "virtual lego" that fosters creativity in its user whereas Microsoft Office is software tool meant to encourage productivity and efficiency, notably characteristics lauded

---

[254] *Ibid.*
[255] Thompson, *supra* note 226 at 119.
[256] *Ibid.*
[257] *Ibid.* at 128.
[258] *Supra* note 203 at 70.

and embodied by Bill Gates. The former places the user in the role of artistic creator; the latter suggests the user is merely an extension of the software itself. Importantly, *Oop!* is applicable in the professional realm as well as it is "usable by scientists, animators, contractors and architects."[259] *Oop!*'s slogan, "*Build every possible universe with Oop!*" is as symbolic as the software itself because it suggests that the use of this software contributes to a professional world other than the one at Microsoft and corporations of that ilk.[260]

Ultimately, it is the potential for creative freedom that lures the Microserfs from their save havens at Microsofts to risk everything at a start-up because at *Oop!* they "get a chance to be 'One-Point-Oh'" which, in the world of computers means being "the *first* to do the *first* version of something."[261] So, rather than continuing to toil away at code that someone else had invented, and that needs to be continuously updated, the Microserfs opt to be creators rather than labourers. Or, as they frame it, "we had to ask ourselves, '*Are you One-Point-Oh?*' – the answer is what separates the Microserfs from the Cyberlords."[262]

Oop!, although dramatically different from Microsoft, is hardly a utopian workplace. On the contrary, it is a company that requires the same grueling hours and sometimes monotonous code testing that made Microsoft unpalatable. As Daniel states, "life has become coding madness all over again," to the point that he and his co-workers euphemistically refer to all-nighters as "flights to Australia," suggesting such intense stints occur frequently enough to merit a nickname.[263] At issue, however, is not so much the workload itself, but the environment and the ideology behind the work. While working for Michael at *Oop!* can prove as exhausting as working for Gates at Microsoft, Daniel clarifies that "*this* time we're killing ourselves for our*selves*, instead of some huge company to whom we might as well be interchangeable bloodless PlaySkool figurine units."[264] Notably, this change in workplace ideology, and their newly found creative autonomy inspires positive change in other avenues of their lives, including physical activity. After weeks of attending a gym, something he never did while at Microsoft, Dan states that "Karla and I are both looking better."[265]

---

[259] *Ibid*. at 72.
[260] *Ibid*.
[261] *Ibid*. at 89.
[262] *Ibid*.
[263] *Ibid*. at 135.
[264] *Ibid*.
[265] *Ibid*. at 290.

"Brought to You By": The Function of Commodification in *Microserfs*

Having traded the punishing regime of Microsoft for the more fulfilling atmosphere at *Oop!*, the Microserfs spend their newly found, though still somewhat limited, leisure time discussing other issues associated with late capitalism which still plague them, such as the pervasiveness of advertising. Such preoccupation with, and consternation about, these elements of commercial culture further aligns them with the protagonists of *Generation X*. The Microserfs' anxiety about the ubiquity of commodification serves a dual purpose. First, it establishes them as members of Generation X, despite their auspicious financial and professional situation. Second, that most of their concerns are articulated after they leave Microsoft demonstrates how their new positions at *Oop!* provide them with an additional, and critical perspective necessary to critique contemporary culture.

Advertising, which functions as the unofficial language of late capitalism, plays a pivotal role in the commodification process to the extent that Susan proclaims, "if Surrealism was around today, it'd last about ten minutes and be stolen by ad agencies to sell long-distance calls and aerosol cheese products."[266] Daniel's observations about the ubiquity of advertising reinforce Jameson's assertion that capitalism, and the commodification that ensues, truly is omnipresent:

> I have noticed that on TV, all of these 'moments' are sponsored by
> corporations, as in '*This touchdown was brought to you by the brewers of*
> *Bud Lite*' or '*This nostalgia flashback was brought to you by the proud*
> *makers of Kraft's family of fine foods.*[267]

The instruments of capitalism are no longer relegated to conventional thirty-second commercials; their reach now extends into moments of the program itself, rendering advertising and product placement inescapable. His concern about "allowing the corporate realm to invade the private" in this manner is similar to the anxiety expressed by Elvissa in *Generation X* about the corporate infiltration of memory in *Generation X*.[268] In terms of this corporate co-opting of memory, advertising is so pervasive that even the promotional mug Karla obtains at her high school reunion is not exempt from "horizontally cross-marketed merchandise tie-ins" thanks to "some

---

[266] *Ibid.* at 44.
[267] *Ibid.* at 131.
[268] *Ibid.*

company in Texas that helps you market your reunion."[269] Disconcertingly, Karla had not really noticed her mug was a portable, ceramic advertisement, and her imperviousness causes Dan to warn ominously, "Beware of the corporate invasion of private memory."[270]

Advertising does not just encroach upon televised programs and souvenirs; its reach expands into the conceptual realm as well. Karla suggests that it will make political participation a question of purchased performativity that functions semiotically as a declaration of ideological allegiance: "I think politics is soon going to resemble a J. Crew catalogue more than some 1776 ideal" wherein one can shop for the most desirable affiliation, and then purchase the material goods necessary to express this allegiance.[271]

Microserfs, like *Shampoo Planet* and *Generation X*, depicts the process of the commodificaiton of history as a result of the rise of advertising, which renders periods of history accessible by purchasing the products associated with a particular era. The Microserfs implicate The Gap, a major clothing retailer, in this very process:

> Just look at the recent "Khakis of the Dead" campaign . . . By using Balanchine and Andy Warhol and all these dead people to hustle khakis, the Gap permits Gap wearer to dissociate from the *now* and enter a nebulous *then* . . . this big place that stretches from Picasso's '20s to the hippie '60s.[272]

The mention of hippies here invokes Moore's observations about the commodification of the sixties in *Shampoo Planet* and Daisy's association with the "McDead," much to her mother's chagrin.

Before their move to California, the Microserfs have a "Zen-o-thon" in an attempt to "shake ourselves of all our worldly crap and become minimalists," a gesture that recalls the aims of Andy, Claire, and Dag.[273] As Bud declares, gleefully having sold his collection of Elle MacPherson merchandise, "This is so 'Zenny.'"[274] Their "Zen-o-thon" is framed ironically because it indicates that the minimalism espoused in *Generation X* has itself become a

---

[269] *Ibid*. at 177.
[270] *Ibid*.
[271] *Ibid*. at 261.
[272] *Ibid*. at 269.
[273] *Ibid*. at 94.
[274] *Ibid*.

commodified identity option, thus gibing at the piety of the protagonists in that novel. Furthermore, the word "Zen-o-thon" recalls the discussion of "telethons" in *Shampoo Planet*. In this case, their garage sale, the most mundane of all rituals, takes on a hackneyed significance as it is, ironically, supposed to be propelling them to a higher plane of existence. Importantly however, Coupland only ironizes the way in which they prepare for their journey to Silicon Valley, but not the decision to move itself because such a decision bespeaks the Microserfs' attempt to rid themselves of the ironic alienation that plagued them at Microsoft.

An Ending Without Irony

The novel's happy, or perhaps even sappy, ending indicates the triumph of Coupland's sentimental authorial personality over the sardonic one. In so doing, it also reconfigures the earlier anxiety about the mechanization of humans in a positive light. This reversal cunningly employs irony in a redeeming and reaffirming manner. When Daniel's mother suffers a stroke and is unable to communicate, Michael suggests hooking her damaged body to a computer so that "the touch of her fingers could be connected to a keypad" thus enabling her to "speak to us."[275] This different type of mechanization restores, rather than compromises, the humanity of Mrs. Underwood, whose dead, "fishy" eyes it hurts Daniel so much to see, and whose body is "all wired up and gizmo'ed" to the extent that "her outside looks like the inside of a Bell switchbox."[276] While the invasion of her body by technology makes her more machine than mother, this is the only way she can express her emotions, an ability endowed with the utmost importance in Coupland's literary mission to forsake ironic detachment. That she uses technology to do this signifies an inversion of the previously discussed "nerd dream" where mechanized humans do not need to address emotions because it is technology itself that enables her to express herself. She quickly re-establishes herself as a mother and wife, rather than a machine, by communicating the nickname she invented for her husband on their honeymoon, and Daniel's distaste for peanut butter in his school lunches.[277] By the end of this scene, all the characters are in tears (and more often than not, the reader is too) and technology has been transformed from a dehumanizing force into a force that enables the expression of emotions, a capacity unique to humans.

---

[275] *Ibid.* at 366.
[276] *Ibid.*
[277] *Ibid.* at 369.

While in *Generation X* and *Shampoo Planet*, ironic detachment resulted from the impossibility of genuine communication using a commodified language, in *Microserfs*, the characters' alienation stems from their jobs at a corporation whose practices dehumanize them and make it difficult for them to "have a life."[278] While at first, this lack of emotion is celebrated as the goal of an efficient nerd vision embodied by Bill Gates, this chapter has demonstrated how the Microserfs transcend this estrangement and the irony that accompanies it by leaving Microsoft to work for *Oop!* where their creativity, rather than their efficiency, is prized. This shift in turn inspires further development in other aspects of their lives which were sorely neglected at Microsoft, such as their physical health and their emotional connections with other human beings. As the novel's ending demonstrates, the Microserfs transcend the ironic detachment that once plagued them. Although earlier in the novel technology promotes mechanistic efficiency over humanity, it is also capable of restoring the human capacity for emotional expression it tried to expunge in another guise. Therefore, *Microserfs* represents a step forward in Coupland's novelistic trajectory because whereas irony is employed at a structural level in *Generation X* to undermine the protagonists' attempt to rise above it, the comparable quest undertaken by the Microserfs is unscathed in this regard. *Microserfs*, then, functions as the penultimate phase in Coupland's novelistic trajectory: it depicts a successful attempt to transcend irony, an objective the protagonist of *Generation X* are unable to accomplish, but this implicit triumph is still one step away from the bombastic challenge wielded against irony in *Girlfriend in a Coma*.

---

[278] *Ibid.* at 27.

Chapter 4 – It's the End of the (Postmodern) World as We Know It:
Girlfriend in a Coma

Like the three novels discussed in the preceding chapters, *Girlfriend in a Coma* is a novel in which Coupland explores his "perennial anxieties regarding the direction of the western world."[279] *Generation X*, *Shampoo Planet*, and *Microserfs*, are all novels that show, with varying degrees of subtlety, how Coupland's writing problematizes postmodern irony. *Girlfriend in a Coma*, however, is anything but tenuous in its renunciation of it, offering nothing less than a forthright dismissal of the apathy and detachment that is biblical in proportion. Through the adoption of a pseudo-religious framework, *Girlfriend in a Coma* is an apocalyptic parable that foretells the end of ironic alienation and the beginning of affective, and therefore effective, engagement with the modern world. The explicit shift towards this philosophical, introspective point of view can, at least in part, be attributed to the deep depression Coupland experienced from 1996-98.[280] However, as chapters 1-3 also illustrate, such a frank disavowal of postmodern irony has nevertheless been gradually percolating throughout his earlier novels.

The opening line of *Girlfriend in a Coma*, "I'm Jared, a ghost," signifies a dramatic shift in gears for Coupland because it immediately introduces how the novel incorporates "the supernatural within an otherwise recognizable contemporary landscape."[281] Jared, the spirit of a 17-year old high school football star who was high school friends with the novel's characters, died young after a battling leukemia. After introducing himself, he explains, retrospectively, that the world has already ended and in order to understand how this predicament unfolded, "we need to learn about [his] friends" who, strangely enough, are the sole inhabitants of this lonely, post-apocalyptic planet.[282] The friends to whom he refers are Karen, Richard, Pam, Hamilton, Wendy, and Linus.

Of these six characters, Karen McNeil emerges as the most pivotal to the novel because the coma she falls into, and miraculously wakes up from, functions as *Girlfriend in a Coma's* primary trope through which a commentary on the perniciousness of postmodern irony is offered. Her character is based on the real-life story of Karen Ann Quinlan, a teenager from New

---

[279] Tate, *supra* note 2 at 328.
[280] Mallick, Heather. "Wakeup Call to Our 90's Coma." *London Free Press* 21 Mar. 1998. *Lexus-Nexus*. InfoTrac. MacLennan Library, McGill University, Montreal, QC. 01 Nov. 2004.
[281] Tate, *supra* note 2 at 335, Coupland, *Girlfriend in a Coma*. Toronto: HarperCollins, 1998 at 1.
[282] *Ibid.* at 5.

Jersey who also lapsed into a coma after combining small doses of alcohol and valium at a party. Quinlan died in 1985 after remaining unconscious for ten years. Her death enabled the media to popularize the "right to die" debate that has continued since.[283] Borrowing heavily from her story, Coupland indulges in literary make-believe by making his Karen wake up 17 years later. This "Rip Van Winkle plot device," Marchand contends, is something that "allows Coupland to put 18 years of social change in dramatic perspective."[284] Karen is the only character able to provide an objective commentary on how the world has changed, because the rest of the novels' characters – Pam, Linus, Wendy, Hamilton, and Richard, having adapted to these changes slowly, are not capable of perceiving their profundity. As Forshaw affirms, Karen's coma provides her with a "unique perspective on the modern world of the 1990s" and as such she enables Coupland to aggressively sketch the "dehumanizing and ultimately pointless accelerated capitalism" that develops in her absence.[285]

The beginning of Karen's coma coincides with the end of a decade, but not just any decade, as the seventies signaled the emerging domination of ideas about postmodernism and late capitalism.[286] Coupland characterizes this change as follows: "And so the time came. The seventies were over. With them left a sweetness, a gentleness. No longer could modern citizens pretend to be naïve."[287] That Karen's coma occurs at a time when the world was poised to change so dramatically makes her an ideal person to describe these developments.

Prior to falling unconscious, Karen struggles to tell her boyfriend Richard, with whom she has just had sex for the first time, the strange visions she has been privy to, and whose meaning utterly confounds her. She sees images like "barely developed photographs," which she thinks reflect "the future," a time when "Russia isn't an enemy anymore. And sex is – fatal."[288] She finds these images quite troublesome because there is a "darkness to the future" to which she and her friends will be impervious. Karen's visions also inform her that she and her friends are the only people left on Earth, although the status of this putatively elevated position is

---

[283] Marchand, *supra* note 47 at 2.
[284] *Ibid.*
[285] *Supra* note 3 at 46.
[286] Nicol, *supra* note 6 at 5.
[287] *Supra* note 281 at 46.
[288] *Ibid.* at 11.

undermined by the fact that she refers to their lives as "meaningless" and describes them as having eyes "without souls . . . like a salmon lying on a dock, one eye flat on the hot wood."[289]

In the final section of the novel, after Karen awakens from her coma, the visions that she had prior to it come to fruition: everyone on the planet dies except for her and her friends. And, just like she predicted, they are apathetic towards their miraculous position as the sole survivors. Frustrated by their detached alienation, Jared reappears, and after berating them for their jadedness, he introduces "Plan B," which is the name he gives to the changes the characters will try to affect in their newly assigned roles as disciples who will rebuild the world according in an introspective and inspiring image so as to rescue it from the state of ironic detachment into which it has fallen. The only downside to "Plan B" is that it requires a sacrifice, and Karen, in a Christ-like gesture, opts to return to her coma as doing so will enable her friends to carry on their mission of transforming the world into a place where wonder trumps apathy and irony is no longer the dominant idiom.

According to Andrew Tate, Coupland's employment of this Judeo-Christian framework makes *Girlfriend in a Coma* a novel that "represents a serious attempt to read an apparently godless world in spiritual terms."[290] In this secular realm, Coupland audaciously positions himself "as the postmodern 'God.'"[291] As such, he is a benevolent deity who not only saves his characters from the death succumbed to by the rest of the world's population, but he also provides them with a chance for redemption, provided they cast aside their ironic worldview. Much like the Judeo-Christian God who felt that a planetary flood was the only way to save a corrupted world and to rebuild it anew, Coupland feels as though a comparable catastrophe is necessary in order to rid the world of the crippling apathy and irony of late capitalism. *Girlfriend in a Coma* therefore invokes this biblical flood and "like Noah and his family," the novel's cast of characters "are chosen to survive, and, in turn, are commissioned with the task of renewing the world."[292] Although such a move seems hubristic, *Girlfriend in a Coma* is a manifesto in which Coupland earnestly calls for the end of the irony his work so closely aligns with late capitalism, and the beginning of a world that prizes wonder over apathy, and celebration over cynicism.

---

[289] *Ibid.* at 12.
[290] *Supra* note 2 at 327.
[291] *Ibid.* at 336.
[292] *Ibid.* at 334.

Robert McGill suggests that the characters in *Girlfriend in a Coma* are "primarily ciphers in Socratic investigation" in that "the utterance has primacy over the utterer."[293] Accordingly, when Jared, Coupland's appointed archangel, frames the novel as "the story of friends of mine who finally learned their lesson," such sentiments reflect Coupland's line of thinking regarding the importance of overcoming irony rather than Jared's own assessment of his friends' situation.[294] While Jared acts as Coupland's earthly representative, Karen is the figure who provides the most effective example of a figure whose commentary, rather than character, is of the utmost importance because her "innocence is the benchmark of the . . . jadedness and corruption" of her friends."[295]

Comas: Medical Condition or Postmodern Pathology?

In Karen's absence, her friends constantly evaluate their lives, and, more often than not, find them wanting. When the members of the group find themselves precariously trapped in a train tunnel and have to avoid the oncoming train by pressing themselves to the side of the tunnel, Richard asks "What if we were to die right there? What had our lives been? What had our ambitions been? . . . We were young; obviously we wanted meaning from life. I felt a craving for duty, but to what?"[296] This craving for duty is analogous with a desire for a grand narrative that attempts to frame, and explain human life cycles in a way that renders them meaningful, and thus confers a sense of purpose. Such a sentiment similar to those articulated by Todd in *Microserfs,* and those felt by the alienated protagonists of *Generation X.*

Linus's comments about the emergence of comas encapsulate the purpose this condition plays in the novel as a symbol of modern ennui. He explains that comas are "a byproduct of modern living, with almost no known coma patients existing prior to World War Two. People simply died. Comas are as modern as polyester, jet travel, and microchips."[297] This observation is strongly resonant not only in terms of how it illuminates the underlying significance of Karen's coma, but also in how it foreshadows the deep sleep plague to which the entire world, save for these seven friends, falls prey. Comas are a tool that enable Coupland to explicitly address the

---

[293] McGill, Robert. "Sublime Simulacrum: Vancouver in Douglas Coupland's Geography of Apocalypse." *Essays on Canadian Writing* 70 (2000): 252-76 at 272.
[294] *Supra* note 281 at 5.
[295] *Ibid.* at 140.
[296] *Ibid.* at 60.
[297] *Ibid.* at 63.

regressive changes society undergoes while Karen is asleep, as well as to highlight the
somnambulant state of the rest of the novel's characters.

For Richard, existing in a world whose conceptual landscape is dominated by irony and
apathy is analogous to being in a comatose state:

> After some years I realized I'd landed myself a major drinking problem –
> a device for coping with life's endlessly long days. I truly wondered if I
> was in some kind of coma myself, shambling through life with an IV drip
> filled with scotch.[298]

The other characters in this novel anesthetize themselves in different ways, and in so doing
create their own comas which numb them to their nagging suspicious that their lives are devoid
of meaning. Pamela and Hamilton become addicted to heroin, though Hamilton concedes this
drug-induced haze is not an effective way to evade the questions that haunt him about the
purposelessness of his existence. Rather, it functions as a it is a substitute in this regard:
"Heroin's not a meaning, but it *does* make life feel as though life still has possibilities."[299] Wendy
becomes a workaholic doctor, notably choosing a profession that reflects her desire to find a cure
for her own life as well as for her patients. Linus becomes an engineer who quits his job, and
goes on a solitary wilderness voyage, only to return when the larger meaning he seeks continues
to elude him. What these divergent avenues of escape have in common is that none of them
provides the intangible significance these characters seek. Rather, such diversions compensate
for the larger meaning they feel their lives lack. As Wendy declares when the friends reunite,
years later: "where do we fit in, Richard? We're all working. We all have jobs but . . . there's
something missing."[300] What she feels is missing is a narrative, some sort of explicatory
framework that bestows them with a purpose: "We're born; there *must* be a logic – some sort of
plan larger than ourselves."[301]

Her speech is comparable to Todd's proclamation in *Microserfs* regarding the moral
ambiguity of the work he and his friends perform at Microsoft. Although Karla arrives at the
conclusion that the purpose and meaning they seek can at least partially be fulfilled by

---

[298] *Ibid.* at. 71.
[299] *Ibid.* at 95.
[300] *Ibid.* at 79.
[301] *Ibid.*

undertaking more creative work, Wendy is at a complete loss as to how to ameliorate her friends' condition. Hamilton, significantly using a television show as a reference point, also highlights the futility of their situation: "in an evil *Twilight Zone* kind of way there's nothing *else* to choose . . . All other options have evaporated. For most people it's the System or what . . . *death*? There's nothing. There's no way out."[302] While this lack of alternatives recalls the Andy, Claire, and Dag's somewhat futile attempt to circumvent commercial culture in *Generation X,* it also recalls how in the Bible, the cataclysmic flood seems to be God's only alternative. When they have this conversation, little do they know that their very own *Twilight Zone* is about to occur as on "October 31, 1997," after "seventeen years, ten months, and seventeen days," Karen awakens from her coma, astounding those around her.[303]

While You Were Sleeping: The Problematization of Progress

Almost immediately upon coming to, Karen is told how different the world has become when Wendy hurriedly informs her that "We're going to have to move you as soon as possible, Karen. The media's changed quite a bit since 1979 and we don't want them vulturing around you."[304] This observation reveals how the role, and pervasiveness, of the media has increased dramatically while Karen was sleeping. Moreover, in a secular realm, Karen's awakening is as close to a modern-day miracle as the reporters will ever get, hence their aggressive pursuit of coverage.

In a gesture that presciently foreshadows the soporific tendency that will shortly sweep the rest of the planet, one of Karen's first desires upon waking up is to return to her somnolent state by taking a nap: "Hey there, Wendy – I saw you watch me yawn. Don't sweat it. I'm going to be falling asleep soon. But it'll only be *normal* sleep."[305] After her nap, she catches up with her friends who try to fill her in on all she has missed. The most noteworthy developments of the past two decades, according to them, creates a very telling mélange indeed, as the list includes, "the fall of the Berlin Wall, AIDS quilt . . . And then there's crack. Cloning. Life on Mars.

---

[302] *Ibid.* at 155.
[303] *Ibid.* at 111.
[304] *Ibid.* at 121.
[305] *Ibid.* at 121.

Velcro. Charles and Diana. MAC cosmetics."[306] Such highlights suggest that pop culture and cosmetics rival watershed scientific and socio-political events in terms of importance.

Karen is especially struck by the attitudinal austerity with which she is confronted: "There is a *hardness* I'm seeing in modern people . . . [they] are frazzled and angry, desperate about money, and, at best, indifferent to the future."[307] In an observation that recalls the workaholic Microserfs discussed in the previous chapter, Karen notices that,

> the whole *world* seems to be working too hard. [She] seems to remember
> leisure and free time as being important aspects of life, but these qualities
> seem utterly absent from the world she now sees in both real life and on
> TV. Work work work work work work work.[308]

Moreover, she realizes how these materialistic pressures have taken the place of a more conventional religious reverence, much in the way that Bill Gates and Microsoft do in the first part of *Microserfs*:

> *Look at this! Look at this!* People are always showing Karen new
> electronic doodads. They talk about their machines as though they possess
> a charmed religious quality – as if these machines are supposed o
> compensate for their owner's inner feeling.[309]

The underlying pun of Karen's characterization of this new world is quite telling as her statement that she "has seen the changes progress has wreaked" is imbued with overtones of the frequently used colloquialism "wreaking havoc," an expression pejorative in its connotations.[310] Moreover, if the "a" in "wreaked" were to be replaced with a "c," it would further reflect her opinion that progress has "wrecked" the world rather than benefited it. The implications of such a thought process are significant because her dubiousness about the benefits of technology, and about whether the modern world has indeed progressed or regressed during her absence, reflects her disbelief in an enlightenment teleology that assumes progress is always meliorative. Karen's

---

[306] *Ibid.* at 138.
[307] *Ibid.* at 155.
[308] *Ibid.* at 143.
[309] *Ibid.*
[310] *Ibid.* at 153.

admission that "I know – you want me to say how great everything is now, but I can't," sharply calls such a notion into question.[311]

The End of the World Isn't Funny: When Irony Becomes Idiomatic

Like the other novels discussed in this book, *Girlfriend in a Coma* also speaks to the disingenuousness of a modern communication dominated by media sound bytes and the resulting irony. As the friends try to deduce how they ended up as five dissatisfied adults, the discovery that emerges from their conversation concerns not so much what is said, but how it is said. Linus's sharp retort to Hamilton shifts the conversation from one about compromised metaphysical meaning to one about compromised communicative sincerity: "you talk funny . . . You talk in little TV bits. You're never sincere . . .I don't think you've ever had a real conversation in your life."[312] Jameson's theory of the "waning of affect" addresses such alienation by evincing that the omnipresence of media and their artificiality compromises our capacity to feel deeply.[313] The detachment that results from this development is evident when Karen "is trying to describe the collapse of the world to her friends" and, rather than seriously contemplate the momentous, apocalyptic events unfolding around them, they instead respond with "funeral giggles – a protective, ironic coating," which demonstrates the full extent of their detachment from, and apathy towards, contemporary society.[314] This affective gap is also underscored later in the novel when Richard and Karen discuss the implications of the destruction that has befallen them. The only level on which Richard is able to cope with these events is a wry one, and this defense mechanism irks Karen, who, having been in a coma when such alienation became a prevalent social force, is able to respond to the situation in a less jaded fashion: "This is *not* a very good time or place for sarcasm, Richard."[315] His response that sarcasm is "called irony these days" demonstrates how in *Girlfriend in a Coma*, irony is inextricably linked to emotional detachment and alienation and has become idiomatic.

---

[311] *Ibid.* at 155.
[312] *Ibid.* at 83.
[313] *Supra* note 27 at 26.
[314] *Supra* note 281 at 199.
[315] *Ibid.* at 180.

Narrative Channel-Surfing: Television and the Grand Narrative

Perhaps one of the reasons they are so unable to apprehend what has happened to them is the nature of their apocalypse: Hollywood has made many "end-of-the-world" movies, but none in which the world ends as the result of a planet-wide nap. When Richard first realizes that something is going gravely wrong, he gropes for a narrative framework and, tellingly, his mind begins "spooling out plotlines from 1970s sci-fi movies," demonstrating the extent to which television has emerged as the new provider of narrative frameworks.[316] Unable to comprehend what is happening, or how the situation will continue to unfold, he gropes for applicable movie plots. Quite unlike the spectacularism expected from a Hollywood film, this particular plague is characterized by torpor rather than over-the-top explosions:

> people who catch this thing – whatever it is – have this powerful urge to
> sleep, so they lie down wherever they are – in their cars, on the mall
> floors, in the offices. A minute later, they're dead.[317]

That Richard even imagines the apocalypse in such terms in the first place speaks to the internalization of a host of Hollywood films that depict it as such. As Karen, who has been less influenced by television plots, explains, "the world was never meant to end like in a Hollywood motion picture – you know: a chain of explosions and stars having sex amid the fire and teeth and blood and rubies. That's all fake shit."[318]

While television is one of the primary culprits that perpetrates this commodified communication, its influence is pervasive on another level as well in that it functions as a surrogate that compensates for Generation X's lack of grand narratives. Building on Lyotard's theory of the decline of the grand narrative in the postmodern era, G.P. Lainsbury asserts that in a society devoid of grand narratives, television serves a compensatory function by providing a makeshift conceptual framework: "the focal point of Gen X consciousness . . . is television. By default, television becomes for Gen X a replacement for the discredited master narratives of western civilization."[319] While perhaps not as profound as a religious framework or Habermas's Enlightenment Project, television has consequently emerged as the medium through which

---

[316] *Ibid.* at 178.
[317] *Ibid.*
[318] *Ibid.* at 208.
[319] *Supra* note 12 at 235.

contemporary plots or storylines are disseminated. Of course, given the prevalence of advertising, and dubious moral rectitude of many programs, it is not surprising that television has contributed to a more materialistic, artificial, and detached worldview.

Although their world does not end like a Blockbuster film, Hollywood nevertheless forms an integral part of their decline because watching films is how the characters pass the time in their post-apocalyptic world. Rather than interrogate their post-apocalyptic surroundings, and ruminate upon why they were the only ones chosen to survive, Richard and his friends continue to revel in the apathy, cynicism, and materialism that, in Coupland's view, as the ersatz deity of this tale, made the apocalypse necessary in the first place.[320] This is why, according to Robert McGill, *Girlfriend in a Coma* "is not an apocalyptic novel" in the conventional sense because what happens in the aftermath of the apocalypse is more significant than the catastrophic event itself.[321] Therefore, the apocalypse that occurs in *Girlfriend in a Coma* is as instructive as it is destructive. Instead of treating the apocalypse, and their seemingly miraculous survival, as a sign that they should rebuild or change their lives, all their energy is subsumed by popular culture. As Richard muses,

> have we ever really gotten together and wished for wisdom or faith to
> come from the world's collapse? No. Instead we got into a tizzy because
> some Leaker[322] forgot to return the *Godfather III* tapes to Blockbuster
> Video the day of the sleep and now we can't watch it.[323]

Jonothan Oakes shares Lainsbury's view that members Generation X's apprehension of "contemporary social reality may perversely depend on a prior reference to a cinematic or televisual modality in order to constitute itself."[324] The veracity of these critics' ideas in this regard is exemplified by the characters' utter dependence upon television in the wake of the apocalypse. So unable are Pam and Hamilton to contemplate the destruction that surrounds them that they revert into a television fantasy realm in which they pretend to be celebrities on their way to dinner parties: "'We can take it to Babe Paley's place in Bermuda for dinner,' 'It's Jamaica, dear. Who's on the guest list?' 'Twiggy. The Sex Pistols. Jackson Pollock. Linda

---

[320] Tate, *supra* note 2 at 237.
[321] *Supra* note 293 at 270.
[322] Leaker is the term the group adopts to refer to the decomposing dead bodies (222).
[323] *Supra* note 281 at 259.
[324] *Supra* note 19 at 92.

Evangelista.'"[325] Before the apocalypse, they needed heroin to cope; now, popular culture has become their drug of choice as it provides them with a supply of "fantasies" in which they can absorb themselves, rather than face their reality.[326]

Popular culture is so pervasive that its role in the afterlife is the first thing Linus thinks of when contemplating death: "when you die, do you still get to watch TV and read magazines, and see what's happening on Earth? Or do you go someplace where that's not an issue?"[327] Evidently, his heaven is one that includes pop culture because he admits how "it would really bug [him] not to know what the city would look like in a hundred years. Or what my favorite stars would look like fifty years from now."[328]

The parable of Noah's flood is a narrative from which Coupland borrows heavily when narrating his postmodern apocalypse. Curious to assess the astounding situation that has befallen them, "the seven walk through the street, where a rain of stunning proportion turns the sky into a sea . . . Nobody can remember the last time it rained so hard."[329] That none of them is reminded of Noah's ark speaks to the extent to which religious paradigms have disappeared from their conceptual frameworks.

Time for Plan B: Life After Irony

In the final section of the novel, which is also its most daring, Jared returns, a ghost "eternally frozen at age seventeen," sent from above in order to "warn his now middle-aged friends of their own folly and spiritual blindness."[330] That he plays such an advisory role when appearing before his friends after the world has ended, and before a new one has been created, posits him as a adolescent version of John Milton's Raphael who, in Book V of *Paradise Lost* relates to Adam his role in the universe, how he came to be, and what he and Eve must do in order to maintain their prelapsarian status. The first thing he does when returning to earth is express his chagrin at their behaviour:

> take a look at *them* now, will you – one year later: useless sacks of dung
>
> *they* are, slumped around Karen's fireplace watching an endless string of

---

[325] *Supra* note 281 at 221.
[326] *Ibid.*
[327] *Ibid.* at 92.
[328] *Ibid.* at 93.
[329] *Ibid.* at 207.
[330] *Ibid.* at 335.

videos, the floor clogged with Kleenex boxes and margarine tubs
overflowing with diamonds and emeralds, rings and gold bullion a parody
of wealth.[331]

The continued materialistic tendencies that fuel their desire to amass goods and wealth are
somewhat parodic, if not pathetic, given that as the only seven people left on the planet, certainly
such valuables are of no further consequence. Apparently, old consumerist habits die hard. The
detritus of the world's materialist inclinations is one of the most poignant aspects of the
apocalypse and it is through this "hodgepodge of debris" that Coupland offers a critique of the
world his characters occupy.[332]

Another aspect of the religious paradigm that underpins this novel emerges when Jared
appears and announces that, "I'm here to speak to you about transforming your lives and
yourselves" thus putting them through a conversion of sorts.[333] Such a proclamation lends
credence to Paul Di Flilppo's assertion that "to call Coupland the John Bunyan of his set would
not be hyperbole."[334] There are definite similarities between this 1998 novel and that 1678
allegory. Indeed, *Pilgrims Progress* is perhaps the most canonical conversion narrative and
Girlfriend in a Coma functions on this level as well because it features "an excoriation of all
banal time-wasters" and puts forth "an urgent appeal to abandon irony and ennui for earnest
engagement with life."[335] Furthermore, while Christian sees a fire that will destroy his town,
Karen sees images that destroy her naïve idealizations of the future. Arguably, the "terrible
Apollyon" against which she and her friends must fight are the cynicism, apathy, and irony of the
late capitalist realm.

Karen and Jared spend a lot of time conversing, and she reveals to him that "I thought
back in 1979 that in the future the world would – *evolve*. I thought that we would make the world
cleaner and safer and smarter."[336] However, as far as she is concerned, "people didn't evolve . . .
people *devolved*."[337] Karen is not the only character whose thoughts and actions provide a

---

[331] *Ibid.* at 211.
[332] McGill, *supra* note 293 at 261.
[333] *Supra* note 281 at 254.
[334] Di Flilppo, Paul. "Douglas Coupland Searching for Salvation in the 70's." *The* Washington Post. 2 Apr. 1998. 1-2.
[335] *Ibid.*
[336] *Supra* note 281 at 217.
[337] *Ibid.*

different perspective on how the world has changed; her daughter Megan, to whom she miraculously gives birth while in a coma, serves a similar function. While both women demonstrate how the world has, to use Karen's term, "devolved," Karen does so through her innocence while Megan does so through her jadedness. Demographically, Karen is able to recall a time before the "dark" future she accidentally envisioned became a reality; Megan, on the other hand, was born when this darkness was beginning to envelop society. As a result, she "had the least formed personality of the group as the world shut itself down, and she is also the least affected by everything."[338] Notably, when she describes the apocalypse herself, Megan says "It was kind of like the whole *world* went into a coma," but she is quick to point out "I'm used to that," thus demonstrating she grew up in a more affectively challenged environment than her parents and their friends.[339]

After this first visit, Jared returns for a second time, this time to play a much more proactive role in changing his friends' behaviour, rather than merely observing it. He scolds them for their indifference and apathy and tells them "you ought to have been squabbling twenty-four hours a day for all of this time – and asked a million questions about why the world became the way it did."[340] This new inquisitive outlook is an integral part of "Plan B," the unironic blueprint for the post-apocalyptic world, which Jared outlines as follows:

> Every day for the rest of your lives, all of your living moments are to be
> spent making others aware of this need – the need to probe and drill and
> examine and locate the words that take us beyond ourselves.[341]

Indeed, Plan B involves introspection, inquisitiveness, and soul-searching of evangelical proportions. Most importantly, Plan B fills the narrative void bemoaned by the characters earlier in the novel: "In your old lives you had nothing to live for. Now you do."[342] In fact, "what Jared is offering the group here is a way out, not just from their post-apocalyptic predicament, but also from out of the ubiquitous *uncertainty* of life in the postmodern era."[343]

---

[338] *Ibid*. at 226.
[339] *Ibid*. at 231.
[340] *Ibid*. at 259.
[341] *Ibid*. at 272.
[342] *Ibid*. at 272.
[343] Forshaw, *supra* note 3 at 51.

As Jared instructs them, "if you're not spending every waking moment of your life radically rethinking the nature of the world . . . then you're wasting your day."[344] However, Plan B, which involves nothing less than an affective makeover on a worldwide scale, requires a steep sacrifice: Karen. Serving as a Christ figure, she will have to permanently return to her coma, or give her life in order to save mankind. Like Jesus, she insists that "Sacrifices need to be made. This is mine."[345] However, in return for this sacrifice, she earnestly tells her friends: "I'm counting on you guys to change the world."[346]

The novel ends optimistically, with Richard stating convincingly that "there must be all of these people everywhere on Earth, eager, no *desperate* for just the smallest sign that there is something finer or larger or more miraculous about ourselves than we had supposed."[347] He and his friends, the disciples of the new world in which they will espouse introspection rather than irony, will help these people find this framework. These post-apocalyptic apostles are charged with the task of remaking a world that centres on questions and enthusiasm, not detachment and apathy. The final words of the novel belong to Richard who, bolstered by newfound convictions, claims that:

> You'll soon be seeing us walking down your street, our backs held proud .
> . . We'll be begging passersby to see the need to question and question and
> question and never stop questioning until the world stops spinning. We'll
> be adults who smash the tired, exhausted system. We'll crawl and chew
> and dig our way into a radical new world. We will change minds and souls
> from stone and plastic into linen and gold – that's what I believe. That's
> what I know.[348]

Are the Critics Jaded Too?

Heather Mallick is accurate in claiming that in *Girlfriend in a Coma*, Coupland is "trying nothing less than to explore the meaning of life."[349] However, that she immediately implores people not to "wince," after making this assertion suggests that the critics are as uncomfortable

---

[344] *Supra* note 281 at 275.
[345] *Ibid.* at 277.
[346] *Ibid.* at 279.
[347] *Ibid.* at 283.
[348] *Ibid.* at 284.
[349] Mallick, Heather. "Wakeup Call to Our 90's Coma." *London Free Press* 21 Mar. 1998. *Lexus-Nexus*. InfoTrac. MacLennan Library, McGill University, Montreal, QC. 01 Nov. 2004.

with probing deeply into the emotional realm as Coupland's characters. The nature of such comments exemplifies the critical wall Coupland is up against. The sheer audacity of *Girlfriend in a Coma* provided much fodder for critics, many of whom were not persuaded by its daring message. Philip Marchand, for example, refers to *Girlfriend in a Coma* not only as "a sermon and a vacuous one," but also, "a literary failure."[350] In the only other thesis that treats *Girlfriend in a Coma*, Alexander MacLeod points to the "reams of negative press this work has attracted" and goes on to suggest that "the most significant commentary on the perceived value of Coupland's work may be the fact that it has been virtually ignored by Canadian scholars."[351] For that matter, with a mere four articles that address it directly, it is a novel that has received scant critical commentary outside of Canada as well.

While perhaps the bad reviews had a role in this dearth of critical analysis, whether one finds it overwrought, brilliantly rendered, or somewhere in the middle, is really beside the point. Regardless of its putative literary shortcomings, *Girlfriend in a Coma* is a novel that demands critical attention because its apocalyptic treatment of postmodernism boldly asks a question that has been latently hovering in the academy for years: what next? How do we move beyond postmodernism? As Mark Forshaw argues, "*Girlfriend in a Coma* is transparently Coupland's bid for serious critical relevance at a time, in the wake of postmodernism's heyday, when people are wondering what comes next."[352] Therefore, although problematic in certain respects, and Forshaw himself concedes that this novel's earnestness and "didacticism" render it rather awkward, nonetheless, the "critique of consumerism, cynicism and complicit postmodern irony" it provides is deserving of scholarly consideration.[353] *Girlfriend in a Coma* makes an imperfect, though admirable, first attempt at responding to such a query.

---

[350] *Supra* note 47.
[351] MacLeod, Alexander. "Between a Rock and a Soft Place: Postmodern-Regionalism in Canadian and American Fiction." Ph.D. Dissertation, McGill University, 2003.
[352] *Supra* note 3 at 56.
[353] *Ibid.* at 57.

Conclusion: X = What?

This book, among the first to address Coupland's first four novels in an attempt to compensate for the lack of critical commentary on his work, has sought to address three interrelated issues: Coupland's antagonistic relationship to postmodernism; how his anxieties in this regard results in a trajectory traced throughout *Generation X*, *Shampoo Planet*, *Microserfs*, and *Girlfriend in a Coma*, in which the ironic alienation that plagues contemporary society is gradually overcome; and how all the characters that strive to repudiate it are part of Generation X.

In Coupland's purview, Generation X is much more than the title of his first novel: it provides a paradigm through which he explores issues associated with late capitalism such as the ubiquity of commodification and the emergence of an ironic idiom that contributes to an alienated worldview, emotional detachment, and a language that has more to do with slogans than sincerity. Coupland's characters are all members of Generation X and thus heavily influenced by these cultural developments. Nevertheless, they do not passively accept the ironic alienation in which these changes have resulted. Rather, they attempt to overcome them.

Each novel discussed in this book represents a different phase in Coupland's journey to transcend postmodern irony. *Generation X* signals his tentative, though paradoxical first step towards such a renunciation. *Shampoo Planet*, vis-à-vis its comprehensive overview of late capitalist alienation reaffirms the importance of such an endeavour in the first place. *Microserfs* is the first novel that implies overcoming irony is indeed possible. Finally, *Girlfriend in a Coma* is Coupland's bold manifesto against the detached cynicism and imperviousness of the contemporary world. Together, these four novels represent the trajectory of an author determined to challenge postmodernism. In so doing, however, Douglas Coupland also puts forth a related challenge, one concerned with revamping the narrow stereotypes surrounding Generation X. So, what does (Generation) X equal? Nothing less than a demographic Coupland reconfigures and commandeers to take on, and ultimately trump, the postmodern condition.

Bibliography

Primary Sources

Douglas Coupland. *Generation X*. New York: St. Martin's, 1991.

---. *Girlfriend in a Coma*. Toronto: HarperCollins, 1998.

---. *Microserfs*. Toronto: HarperCollins, 1995.

---. *Shampoo Planet*. Simon, 1992.

Secondary Sources

Annesley, *Blank Fictions*. London: Pluto, 1998.

Baudrillard, Jean. *Simulacra and Simulation*. Trans. Sheila Faria Glaser. Ann Arbor: U of
    Michigan, 1994.

Coughlin, Ruth. "Coupland: An Elder Statesman." *Chicago Sun-Times* 27 March, 1994: 1-3.
    Lexus-Nexus. InfoTrac. MacLennan Library, McGill University, Montreal, QC. 01 Nov.
    2004.

Daoust, Phil. "Generation ZZZzzzz." *The Guardian*. 22 Apr. 1998. 1-2. *Lexus-Nexus*. InfoTrac.
    MacLennan Library, McGill University, Montreal, QC. 01 Nov. 2004.

Delvaux, Martine. "The Exit of a Generation: The 'Whatever' Philosophy.' *Midwest Quarterly*:
    A Journal of Contemporary Thought 40 (1999): 171-86. *Lexus-Nexus*. InfoTrac.
    MacLennan Library, McGill University, Montreal, QC. 01 Nov. 2004.

Di Flilppo, Paul. "Douglas Coupland Searching for Salvation in the 70's." *The Washington Post*.
    2 Apr. 1998. 1-2.

Dreher, Rod. "Teenagers Go Global in Coupland's *Shampoo Planet*." *The Washington Times* 17
    Sept. 1992. D8.

Eco, Umberto. "Postmodernism, Irony, the Enjoyable." 1985. *Postmodernism and the
    Contemporary Novel: A Reader*. Nicol, Bran, ed. Edinburgh: Edinburgh UP, 2002. 110-
    13.

Epstein, Jonathon S. ed. *Youth Culture: Identity in a Postmodern World*. Massachusetts:
    Blackwell, 1998.

Forshaw, Mark. "Douglas Coupland: In and Out of Ironic Hell." *Critical Survey* 12.3 (2000):
    39-58.

Fussell, Paul. *Class*. New York: Ballantine, 1983.

Gowen, Anne. "Coupland's Coup at Embassy." *The Washington Times* 24 Feb. 1994. C10.

Grassian, Daniel. *Hybrid Fictions*. New York: McFarland, 2003.

Hruska, Bronwen. "Is There Life After Irony for Coupland?" *San Francisco Chronicle* 1 Mar.
1994: 1-3. *Lexus-Nexus*. InfoTrac. MacLennan Library, McGill University, Montreal,
QC. 01 Nov. 2004.

Jameson, Frederic. *Postmodernism or, the Cultural Logic of Late Capitalism*. Durham: Duke UP,
1991.

Jillson, Cal. *Pursuing the American Dream: Opportunity and Exclusion Over Four Centuries*.
Kansas: Kansas UP, 2004.

Lainsbury, G.P. "*Generation X* and the End of History." *Essays on Canadian Writing* 58 (1996):
229-40.

Lohr, Steve. "No More McJobs for Mr. X." *New York Times* 29 May 1994. D11.

Lyotard, Jean François. *The Postmodern Condition: A Report on Knowledge*. Trans. Geoff
Bennington and Brian Massumi. 1979. Minneapolis: U of Minnesota P, 1984.

MacLeod, Alexander. "Between a Rock and a Soft Place: Postmodern-Regionalism in Canadian
and American Fiction." Diss. McGill U, 2003.

Mallick, Heather. "Wakeup Call to Our 90's Coma." *London Free Press* 21 Mar. 1998. *Lexus-
Nexus*. InfoTrac. MacLennan Library, McGill University, Montreal, QC. 01 Nov. 2004.

Marchand, Philip. "Humbleness of the Heart." *Toronto Star* 21 Mar. 1998: M15.

Martin, Catherine E. et al. "Perspectives on Generation X." *Popular Culture Review* 8.2 (1997):
109-19.

McGill, Robert. "Sublime Simulacrum: Vancouver in Douglas Coupland's Geography of
Apocalypse." *Essays on Canadian Writing* 70 (2000): 252-76.

McInerney, Jay. "Geek Love." *The New York Times*. 11 Jun. 1995: 1-3. *Lexus-Nexus*. InfoTrac.
MacLennan Library, McGill University, Montreal, QC. 01 Nov. 2004.

Mills, Katie. "'Await Lightning': How Generation X Remaps the Road Story." Ulrich, John. M.
and Andrea L. Harris, eds. *GenXegesis: Essays on Alternative Youth (Sub)Culture*.
Wisconsin: U of Wisconsin P, 2003. 221.-49.

Milton, John. "Paradise Lost." *The Riverside Milton*. Ed. Roy Flannagan. Boston: Houghton
Mifflin Company, 1998. 297-711.

86

Moore, Ryan. "And Tomorrow Is Just Another Crazy Scam': Postmodernity, Youth and the Downward Mobility of the Middle Class." *Generations of Youth: Youth Cultures and History in Twentieth Century America*. Eds. Joe Austin, and Michael Nevia Willard. New York: U of New York P, 1998. 326-38.

Muecke, D.C. *The Compass of Irony*. London: Methuen, 1969.

Nicol, Bran, ed. *Postmodernism and the Contemporary Novel: A Reader*. Edinburgh: Edinburgh UP, 2002.

Oake, Jonathon I. "*Reality Bites* and Generation X as Spectator." *The Velvet Light Trap* 53 (2004): 83-97.

Revenge of the Nerds. Dir. Jeff Kanew. 20th Century Fox, 1984.

Rushkoff, Douglas. *The GenX Reader*. New York: Ballantine, 1994.

Samuel, Lawrence R. *Brought To You By: Postwar Television Advertising and The American Dream*. Austin: U of Texas P, 2001.

Segal, David. "An Empty Tale of Modern Times." *The Washington Post* 13 Jul. 1995: 1-2. *Lexus-Nexus*. InfoTrac. MacLennan Library, McGill University, Montreal, QC. 01 Nov. 2004.

Tate, Anthony. " 'Now – here is my secret': Ritual and Epiphany in Douglas Coupland's Fiction." *Literature and Theology* 16.3 (2002): 326-38.

Tebbel, John. *From Rags to Riches: Horatio Alger, Jr. and The American Dream*. New York: MacMillan, 1963.

Thompson, Graham. "'Frank Lloyd Oop': *Microserfs*, Modern Migration and the Architecture of the Nineties." *Canadian Review of American Studies* 31.3 (2001): 119-35.

Ulrich, John M. and Andrea L. Harris, eds. *Gen-X-Egesis: Essays on Alternative Youth (Sub)Culture*. Madison: U of Wisconsin P, 2003.

Works Consulted

Adorno, Theodor. *The Culture Industry: Selected Essays on Mass Culture*. New York: Routledge, 2001.

Aronowitz, Stanley, et al. *Technoscience and Cyberculture*. New York: Routledge, 1996.

Baker, Stephen. *The Fiction of Postmodernity*. Boston: Rowman & Littlefield, 2000.

Bauman, Zygmunt. *Postmodernity and its Discontents*. New York: New York UP, 1997.

Behler, Ernst. *Irony and the Discourse of Modernity*. Seattle: U of Washington P, 1990.

Best, Steven and Douglas Kellner. *Postmodern Theory: Critical Interrogations*. New York: Guilford, 1991.

---. *The Postmodern Turn*. New York: Guilford, 1997.

Betts, Raymond F. *A History of Popular Culture: More of Everything, Faster and Brighter*. New York: Routledge, 2004.

Connor, Steven. *Postmodernist Culture: An Introduction to Theories of the Contemporary*. Oxford: Blackwell, 1989.

Fiddes, Paul S. *The Promised Land: Eschatology in Theology and Literature*. Massachusetts: Blackwell, 2000.

Flory, Richard W. and Donald E. Miller. *Gen X Religion*. New York: Routledge, 2000.

Freese, Peter and Charles B. Harris. *The Holodeck in the Garden: Science and Contemporary American Fiction*. Dalkey Archive, 2004.

Grenz, Stanley J. *A Primer on Postmodernism*. Michigan: W.B. Eerdmans, 1996.

Grossberg, Lawrence. *We Gotta Get Out of this Place: Popular Conservatism and Postmodern Culture*. New York: Routledge, 1992.

Hutcheon, Linda. *Irony's Edge: The Theory and Politics of Irony*. New York: Routledge, 1994.

---. *The Politics of Postmodernism*. London: Routledge, 2002.

Loeb, Paul Rogat. *Generation at the Crossroads: Apathy and Action on the American Campus*. New Jersey: Rutgers UP, 1994.

Long, Elizabeth. *The American Dream and the Popular Novel*. New York: Routledge, 1985.

McHale, Brian. *Postmodernist Fiction*. New York: Routledge, 1987.

Natoli, Joseph. *A Primer to Postmodernity*. Oxford: Blackwell, 1997.

Niall, Lucy ed. *Postmodern Literary Theory: An Anthology*. New York: Blackwell, 2000.

Prickett, Stephen. *Narrative, Religion and Science: Fundamentalism versus Irony, 1700-1999*. Cambridge: Cambridge UP, 2002.

Rice, Philip and Patricia Waugh, eds. *Modern Literary Theory*. 4th ed. London: Arnold, 2001.

Teich, Albert H. *Technology and the Future*. Belmont CA: Thomson, 2003.

Wilde, Alan. *Horizons of Assent: Modernism, Postmodernism, and the Ironic Imagination*. Baltimore: Johns Hopkins UP, 1981.

Williams, James. *Lyotard: Towards a Postmodern Philosophy*. Cambridge: Polity Press, 1998.

Printed in the United Kingdom by
Lightning Source UK Ltd., Milton Keynes
141009UK00001B/136/P

Printed in the United Kingdom by
Lightning Source UK Ltd., Milton Keynes
141009UK00001B/136/P

9 783639 045932